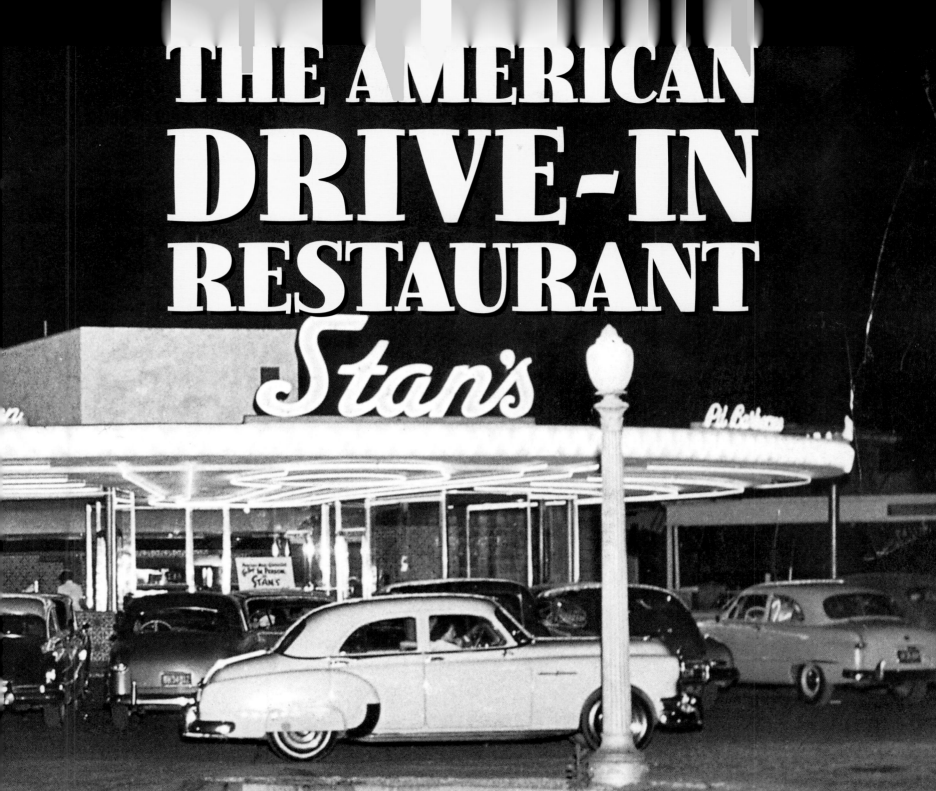

THE AMERICAN DRIVE-IN RESTAURANT

MICHAEL KARL WITZEL

MBI Publishing Company

First published in 1994 by MBI Publishing Company, Galtier Plaza, Suite 200, 380 Jackson Street, St. Paul, MN 55101-3885 USA

© Michael Karl Witzel, 1994, 2002

MBI Publishing Company books are also available at discounts in bulk quantity for industrial or sales-promotional use. For details write to Special Sales Manager at Motorbooks International Wholesalers & Distributors, Galtier Plaza, Suite 200, 380 Jackson Street, St. Paul, MN 55101-3885 USA.

Library of Congress Cataloging-in-Publication Data   ISBN 0-7603-1350-4

On the front cover: The Famous Mel's Drive-In chain once lit up the California night with its neon. Today, as part of the drive-in revival, the Universal Studios theme parks in Hollywood and Orlando pay homage to the drive-in legacy begun by restaurateur Mel Weiss. Both locations feature an idealized re-creation of the now-legendary Mel's Drive-In. *©1992 Universal Studios Florida*

On the frontispiece: The famous Porky's Drive-In in St. Paul, Minnesota. *Michael Dregni.* A well-stacked hamburger meal served with a plate of French fries and extra large Coca-Cola. *Michael Karl Witzel.* Pig Stand carhop Ruth Forke. *Dallas Public Library*

On the title page: Stan's Drive-In, Fresno, California, 1950s. *Courtesy Martin Cable, Edwin Schober photographer*

On the verso and contents page: Walt's Bar Restaurant Grill on US Highway 46 in Essex County, New Jersey, in July 1947. Is there any doubt that this stand was built by an ex-wartime aviator. *Standard Oil (New Jersey) Co. Collection, Photographic Archives, University of Louisville*

On the back cover: Lorraine Magowan worked hard for many years as a carhop at Simon's Drive-In at Wilshire and Santa Monica in Los Angeles, California. *Michael Karl Witzel.* Katson's Drive-In, Albuquerque, New Mexico, circa 1940. *Courtesy Chuck Sturm*

All cover and front-matter images courtesy Coolstock.com Collection.

Printed in Hong Kong

CONTENTS

ACKNOWLEDGMENTS **6**

FOREWORD **8**

INTRODUCTION **9**

Chapter One
AMERICA'S NEW MOTOR LUNCH **12**

Chapter Two
THE CIRCULAR MECCA OF NEON **46**

Chapter Three
NEWER VISIONS FOR ROADFOOD **108**

Chapter Four
DRIVE-IN DEMISE AND RE-RISE **148**

BIBLIOGRAPHY **188**

INDEX **192**

Acknowledgments

A triple decker thanks to the individuals who donated time, knowledge, remembrances, photographs, advertisements, contacts, and suggestions. Most notably, Will Anderson, Nancy Baker, Joan Baxter, Joseph R. Blackstock, Brian Butko, Martin Cable, Pat Chappell, David Clements, Dan Daniels, Mike Dapper, Michael Dregni, Albert Doumar, Tom Duffey, Bill Dushatko, Amy Eliezer, Wanda Faist, Ruth Forke, Ralph Grossman, John Hanks, Frank Haywood, Edith Hoover, Charles K. Hyde, Harvey Kaplan, Jerry Keyser, Eric H. Killorin, Bruce Kraig, Arthur Krim, Mildred "Skeeter" Kobzeff, Pat Krohlow, Philip Langdon, Teresa Linscott, Robert Linscott, Ramona Longpré, Richard Longstreth, Lorraine Magowan, Wayne McAllister, Richard McDonald, Richard McLay, Boe Messett, Tom Morrison, Biff Naylor, Greg Naylor, Victor Newlove, Chris Nichols, Clare Patterson, Jr., Dale Poore, Bill Roberts, Kyle Roberts, Ted Roen, Keith A. Sculle, Louise Sivils, Troy N. Smith, Melba Stapleton, Ronald N. Schneider, Chuck Sturm, Jeffrey Tennyson, Buna "Johnnie" Van Hekken, Buzz Waldmire, Marc Wanamaker, J. Frank Webster, and June Wian.

A generous slice of appreciation is reserved for the stock photo agencies, historical archives, photographers, and artists that supplied images, including Warren Anderson, the Atlanta Historical Society, Inc., Arizona Historical Society, Kent Bash, The Texas Collection at Baylor University, Annabelle Breakey, Burbank Historical Society, the Cambridge Historical Commission, Chicago Historical Society, Culver Pictures, Inc., Craig Curtin, the Dallas Historical Society, Georgia Historical Society, Henry Ford Museum & Greenfield Village, Historical Society of Seattle and King County, Kansas State Historical Society, Karl Korzeniewski, Steven Lewis, The Museum of Modern Art, National Archives, the National Museum of American History, The New York Historical Society, Oregon Historical Society, Los Angeles Public Library Photo Collection, Louis Persat, Personality Photos, Inc., Photosource International, Preziosi Postcards, Quincy Historical Society, Renton Historical Society, the Sacramento Archives & Museum Collection Center, Saline County Historical Society, Security Pacific Historical Photograph Collection, Andy Southard, Jr., Standard Oil of New Jersey Collection, Unicorn Stock Photos, Randy Welborn, and of course, Gabriele Witzel.

An extra-large order of fries should go to the libraries, librarians, and researchers who assisted, namely Kim M. Miller and the Antique Automobile Club of America Library and Research Center, Joan Johnson of Circa Research and Reference, Detroit Public Library,

Carol Roark and the Dallas Public Library, Howard University Libraries, Brita Mach and Jenny Watts of the Huntington Library, The Library of Congress, Caroline Kozo-Cole and Jane Nowak of the Los Angeles Public Library, Michigan State University Library, Spokane Public Library, Laura Barnard and Christine Firth of the Seattle Public Library, Bill Carner and the University of Louisville Ekstrom Library, Dace Taube of the University of Southern California Library, Washington State University Library, and Wichita Public Library.

Without the assistance of certain organizations and associations, this project would have stuck to the grill. "Order up" goes to Christopher Raab of A&W Restaurants, Inc., Karen Johnston of Beatrice/Hunt-Wesson, Elizabeth Eller, Georgia Grove, Lori A. McManes, and Linda Williams of the Coca-Cola Company, Mildred Walker of the Dr Pepper Museum, Michael Dunlavey and Yvonne Guerra of The Dunlavey Studios, Inc., Kathy Lendech of Hanna-Barbera Entertainment Company, the Hot Dog Hall of Fame, Elizabeth Snyder and the Ice Screamers, the Kansas City Museum, Wayne King of Kings-X Inc. and Jimmie's Diner, Katherine Hamilton-Smith and Debra Gust of the Lake County Museum, George Lucas and Lynne Hale of Lucasfilm, Ltd., Joan Costigan and Doris Morris of Marriott Corporation,

Courtesy Metro ImageBase

Jennifer K. Sebree of MCA/Universal Pictures, Steven Weiss and Mels Drive-Ins, Metro Imagebase, Larry Wagerle and the National Association of Soda Jerks, Phillips Petroleum Company, Schiffer Publishing, Ltd., Seaver Center for Western History Research of the Natural History Museum of Los Angeles County, the Society for Commercial Archeology, Nancy Robertson and Sonic Industries, Inc., Janet P. Boston and Steak n Shake, Inc., Rus Riddell and Swensen's Ice Cream, Dwayne Jones of the Texas Historical Commission, Richard Hailey of the Texas Pig Stands, Inc., Linda Tibbetts Buckley of Universal Studios Florida, Susan H. Gordy and Gordon Muir of The Varsity, Inc.

Finally, a special topping of thank yous to my wife, Gyvel Z. Young-Witzel for her tireless editorial assistance, fact-verification, research, accounting services, moral support, and otherwise unsung duties relating to the completion of this project.

Courtesy Gabriele Witzel

FOREWORD

by Philip Langdon

From their beginnings in the 1920s until their astonishingly sudden fall from grace during the 1960s, drive-in restaurants were some of the most spontaneously enjoyable diversions ever produced by American road commerce.

Without giving up the semi-private world of their automobile interior, motorists could summon service simply by flashing their headlights or depressing the switch on a speaker-box. In a flash an eager carhop would arrive—perhaps dressed in a colorful majorette uniform—or in some instances, sporting roller skates. Gliding across the asphalt with a tray full of hamburgers, French fries, and milkshakes, the curb-girl was an unforgettable sight.

The drive-in itself was a youthful vision of paradise. Youth liked its food tasty, moderately priced, and quick—just the way the drive-in served it. Equally important, teens liked their restaurants to have a stimulating atmosphere, and successful operations rarely disappointed on that score. The continual comings and goings of an eclectic caravan of customers made the dining-room-on-a-parking-lot the ideal spot for people-watching, making new friends, confronting rivals, and sparking romance.

Families were beckoned by the magic of the drive-in, too. This was one kind of restaurant where parents could enjoy taking their children—without all the worry about behavior or kids making a mess. Here, personal freedom reigned. Customers of all ages were liberated from the expectations and inhibitions that governed the confining conventions of indoor dining.

The uniquely American experience of the drive-in restaurant reflects the twentieth century's ascent of unprecedented mobility and informal living styles. Whether, in the end, the drive-in exerted a desirable or a disruptive influence on the character of America's highways and cities is debatable. However, there can be no doubt that it mirrored a nation's movement toward mobility, changing the roadways…forever.

Today, the imagery of drive-in dining and all its trappings evoke fond memories. Those were the days of so many pleasurable memories—times of relaxation, times of excitement, times when owning a jalopy was a big thrill, and chomping a burger at one's favorite carhop restaurant was a pleasure.

While many of the classic operations have disappeared, they will not be forgotten. And, for all those nostalgic diners with a yearning for the way things used to be, Michael Karl Witzel's book provides the vehicle to revisit the past—a unique opportunity to experience the taste, sound, and atmosphere of some of America's best drive-in restaurants.

INTRODUCTION

As a small fry growing up in the 'burbs of New Jersey, my palate was yet untouched by fast food and its frozen, prefabricated wares. My eager young tastebuds had only experienced the culinary feasts of Mom and Pop eateries that thrived along the Jersey roadside.

Unique food specialties were still the norm back then—staple entrees influenced by a diverse range of ethnic tastes. From the tall oaks of Ringwood to the beaches of Wildwood, every type of family-operated hamburger, hot dog, pizza, sandwich, or ice cream "joint" could be frequented along the commercial corridors. When it came to the simple preparation of roadfood and serving it up to motorists with a practiced style and braggadocio, New England was thicker than the ketchup made famous by Heinz.

Saturday was the special day my Dad and I reserved to explore those flavorful roadways. Pulling out of the driveway from our suburban outpost we embarked on a mission to indulge in the simple pleasures of the motorcar, spend time together, and secretly sample the best junk food that ever tickled our tastebuds.

Although Mom could cook up a superb sauer braten dish, the addictive lure of roadfood and the magic that it promised to add to our vehicular adventures were an addiction we couldn't resist. Hooked, we pledged our culinary allegiance to the offbeat eateries serving the roadside genre.

Through small townships and boroughs we rolled, a piston-powered juggernaut headed far from the suburban sensibilities of my Mother's home kitchen. Within the confines of

Courtesy Metro ImageBase

Suskana Saran Seat Covers

Automotive seat cover manufacturers demonstrated the stain-resistant properties of their fabrics during the fifties and sixties. For a society in love with their automobiles, it was welcome news. Now, dining in the car—whether that meant greasy hamburgers or drippy ice cream—could be worry-free. Oh, the joys of in-car dining!

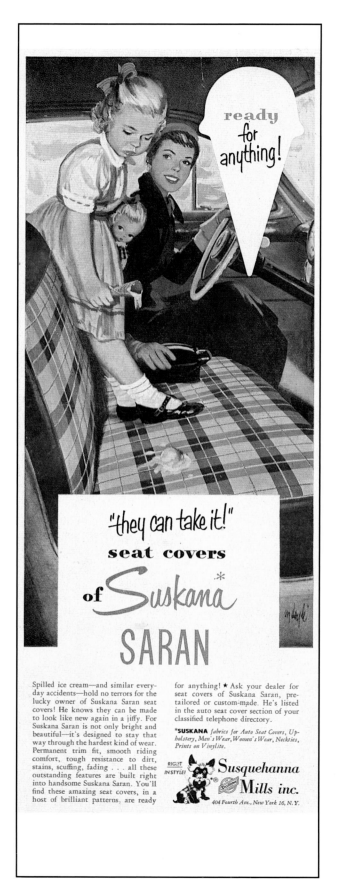

the family automobile, we talked, consuming the visual wonders of the roadway rushing towards us through a curved panorama of glass. Roadfood mecca was waiting for us…just around the bend.

While we scanned the horizon for just the right dining spot, I played many of the games youngsters play within a moving vehicle: pushing radio buttons to rock'n'roll stations my Dad didn't like, imitating race car sounds, and sprinting alongside the car—in my imagination. Not one obstacle on the sidewalk proved a match for my high-speed fantasy jumps.

Sometimes, my flattened palm became airborne. Like a jet plane, it streaked through the air, diving and climbing in the thick airstream flowing by my open window. Intoxicated with the speed of the internal-combustion engine, telephone poles and street signs rushed past in a myopic blur. I fell in love with the road!

The Wanaque Drive-In was always first in line, located just over the town line. A simple structure situated at an angle to the roadway, it beckoned passing customers with three oversized garage doors opened wide. Visible from the roadway, its long serving counter and menu signboard became a backdrop for the silhouettes of happy diners, wolfing grilled delights. Inside, a dozen tiny tables were outfitted with standard-issue salt and pepper shakers. Wooden chairs of every variety set the informal atmosphere with condiment squeeze bottles containing mustard and ketchup providing a decorative splash of color. Without fail, the house specialty was always a classic hot dog, prepared with mounds of fresh kraut and piles of tangy relish. Greedily, my father and I grabbed our orders and headed for the four-wheel dining compartment, content to observe the pageantry of cars and customers as we filled our tummies with tubesteak.

On the rare occasions when we had room left over for dessert, the craving for home-made ice cream set the course for our next stop. Without exception, that meant driving just a few miles down the avenue to our favorite outlet for frozen treats: the Milk Barn.

A one-of-a-kind establishment dedicated to ice cream, it was covered in weathered cedar shingles and featured an oversized parking lot. Inside, the cavernous interior held dozens of roomy booths and oversized picnic tables. Riddled with knot holes and other imperfections, all were constructed of thick wood. Every visible surface was deeply engraved with thousands of messages carved by an uncountable procession of patrons. Heavy layers of shellac made possible all variety of graffiti, from generic, friendly greeting to undying pledge of love.

While sitting at one of the tables licking a double-scoop cone of chocolate almond or devouring a banana split deluxe, it was easy to let imaginations drift. Whatever became of the people who left behind hand-scrawled triptychs such as "Johnny Loves Suzy," "Greetings from Fort Lee," or "The Andersons were here January 14, 1967"?

At the Milk Barn, the inborn desire to leave proof behind of one's visit and make a mark on the physical realm created a unique dining atmosphere. More important, it gave what would have normally been just a great roadside ice creamery real soul.

Sometimes, we would forego the hot dog and ice cream routine and save our appetites for pizza. Larry's had its share of character, too—but there, the food commanded our complete attention. With no regard for indigestion or abdominal distress, we eagerly coated twenty-five-cent wedges of cheese with copious amounts of red pepper sprinkles and hot yellow seed! A large Pepsi washed down the saucy snack as we gazed in awe at the Old World pizza master pounding, flipping, massaging, and pulling raw dough into the edible product we revered.

Silently, the flabby disc twirled in the air, assumed a perfect shape, then landed, a light breath of flour exhaling from its final contact with the marble. It was magic! With a graceful flourish, Larry—or one of his sons, or brothers, or cousins, or uncles—ladled a healthy dollop of tomato sauce upon the flattened bread. In an ever-widening spiral, he carefully coated the pie in preparation for the generous shower of mozzarella that followed. As we devoured our triangles, we watched it all with reverent silence, hypnotized by the culinary miracle of new pies being born.

Eventually, I outgrew those weekend journeys with my Dad and assumed my rightful place behind the steering wheel among the machines on the highway. The trials of growing up and the demands of everyday living edged out the leisure time once used to watch a pizza man work. Still, I look back fondly on those wonderful times and feel fortunate that the formative years of my streetside schooling included the distinctive restaurant operations we discovered together.

I learned well from them all, memorizing the boomerang patterns of their tabletop Formica, consuming the whimsy of their homemade billboards, etching the twisted traces of their colorful neon into memory. To this day, the swirling imagery of ice cream cones, Coca-Cola buttons, polished diners, fruit stands, advertising mascots, drive-in theaters, carhop restaurants, lunch counters, freeway exits, intersections, and the occasional glimpse of an abandoned automobile take me way, way back to those flavorful days of my youth.

Michael Karl Witzel
Wichita, Kansas
August 1993

AMERICA'S NEW
MOTOR LUNCH

Once upon a time in the far, distant past over one hundred years ago—long before there were any plans devised for McDonald's, Wendy's, Burger King, Little Caesars, Carl's Junior, Kentucky Fried Chicken, Whataburger, Jack in the Box, Hardee's, Roy Rogers, or even Taco Bell—the acts of traveling and dining were still considered separate events.

For the most part, the horse-drawn covered wagon proved to be an impractical vehicle for dining on the go. Early carriage designs made no accommodation for beverage holders, and there was no safe place to clip a serving tray. Similarly, four-hoofed transport atop a saddle provided little convenience or comfort when it came to breaking sourdough. While horses were well suited to graze freely of grasses along the route, hungry drovers fared best to ignore hunger pangs until dismount.

When all the frontiers were finally conquered and the population began to fill in the space between each coast, trains, carriages, and horse-drawn travel were overtaken by an economical motorcar for everyone. Once Hen-

ry Ford eliminated the kinks from his assembly line operation in 1913 and set the course to replace the iron horse, mobile dining conditions promised to improve. Now, instead of relying on a train line's "butcher boy," the proud owners of a Model T could strap their picnic baskets onto the running board, throw Junior into the backseat, and motor as far and wide as a tank full of gasoline would take them.

Despite the newfound mobility promised by the automobile and its undeveloped potential for dining, there were still limited choices to consider when thoughts of passenger and pilot turned to food. Of course, there was the occasional wayside inn or resort hotel with dining facilities, but with roads still undeveloped, conveniences "out in the sticks" were largely unheard of. Once the limited buffer zone of civilization surrounding a town was breached, automobilists were on their own until they reached the next settlement or nearest grove of fruit trees. In the days when gasoline was purchased from depots on the outskirts of town, refined dining establishments were often as scarce as a fuel pump.

Not surprisingly, planning ahead also became the watch words for those anticipating any sort of meal along secluded routes. A small wicker basket filled to the brim with dishes, silverware, and the foods normally reserved for the sit-down supper became part of many journeys. Containing an overflow of home-cooked goodies such as fried chicken, pork chops, and a loaf of bread, the picnic basket was the portable larder to feed the family on the go. To that end, it wasn't always necessary to stop: sandwiches could be eaten and drinks chugged from a bottle in the front seat—even while the pistons popped!

Realistically, Sunday sightseers and cross-country vacationers made up only a small percentage of the growing rabble of motorists taking to the roadways. Despite Ford's reduction in auto prices, the majority of motorized Americans were working hard just to keep up

continued on page 18

In the far, distant past over one hundred years ago, the acts of traveling and dining were still considered separate events. Despite the newfound mobility promised by the automobile, there were still limited choices when thoughts of passenger and pilot turned to food.

Roadside Picnic Table Scene
Former Farm Security Administration photographer John Vachon froze the family picnic for future study while visiting High Point State Park in Sussex County, New Jersey, in June 1947. Although drive-in eateries were common during that era, the family picnic on the side of the road was just as enjoyable. There was less car exhaust, and a lot less noise. Standard Oil (New Jersey) Co. Collection, Photographic Archives, University of Louisville

SPLENDOR OF THE SODA FOUNTAINS

When the temperance movement forced many states to prohibit the sale of liquor during the 1870s, America's parched populace began turning to the corner drugstore for relief. Eager for liquid refreshment, it was only natural that their search would lead them to the friendly pharmacist: after all, he was once the leading dispenser of alcohol.

Soda Fountain
Walgreen Drugs was one of the Midwest's largest drugstores chains during the late twenties. Not only did they feature fountain service, many had lunch counters that could serve well over a hundred people per hour. In 1929, Ray Kroc, salesman for the newly merged Lily and Tulip Cup Company, approached Walgreen Drugs with a revolutionary new concept—carryout food! By replacing their current glassware with disposable cups, folks could order "to go" shakes and drinks. Walgreen's business doubled and ten years later they were convinced (once more) to try a new concept—this time it was the rapid-action Multimixer. Hedrich-Blessing photograph. Courtesy the Chicago Historical Society

Pharmacy owners lost no time in acclimating to the new situation. By heavily promoting carbonated beverages, an all-out campaign was launched to regain revenues lost from alcohol sales. Obsolete liquor advertising signs were tossed regretfully into the storage room. Oversized display racks were hastily removed, too, clearing way for tables and chairs.

To entice new patronage, the creation of cozy conversation areas became an integral part of the revamped marketing plan. Now, folks could linger—all while sipping the effervescent liquids produced by the Lippincott and Puffer fountains.

Eventually, the competition that followed spurred many drugstore operators to construct elaborate fountain areas. Gleaming counters of marble and alabaster replaced homely wood. Ornate mirrors and lamps added an air of elegance. Crafted in the form of goddesses, gargoyles, and sphinxes, intricate spigots yielded sparkling fluid with a turn of the wrist. This union of polished stone and mirrored back bar soon became an integral part of the modern drugstore.

To America's alcohol-deprived, the effect of fountain drinks and sundaes was one of deep satisfaction. Who could resist carbonated waters blended with ice cream, syrups, marshmallows, and nuts? At long last, the public's parboiled palates were quenched! Fantasy mixtures like the "Catawba Flip," "Panama Cooler," and "Black-Eyed Susan" became popular tonics of the era.

Commanding the spigots was a new youthful wonder: the soda jerk. With his skillful manipulations, generous supplies of whipped cream and syrup joined with the bubbling waters. Highly coveted, his position was the product of many months, and sometimes years, of menial tasks performed around the store. As consummate showman, innovator, and freelance linguist of the drugstore stage, America's soda jerk became the pop culture star of the Gilded Age.

As fountain popularity swelled, many drugstores lacked the interior space to accommodate the onslaught. To handle the rush, young curb servers soon joined the soda jerks. Visionary operators determined that the lads could deliver soda fountain creations outside to the waiting buggies. Since they were paid by customers' tips, the monetary risk was minimal. Without moving or remodeling, the drugstore operator could increase sales volume and convenience.

Within a short time, curbs were lined with carriages. Energetic curb servers relayed requests for a "barked pie" (with upper crust), one "in the hay" (strawberry shake), and Java to the inside soda jerk—all prepared to "go for a walk."

Unfortunately, this leisurely style of ice cream parlour service eventually gave way to the bustling frenzy of drive-ins and walk-up fast-food stands. Flamboyant soda jerks were replaced by grill men and fry cooks. Assembly-line burgers became the new art form. Soon, curb boys sporting cow-licks were dumped for carhops in form-fitting fashions.

As the exodus to the suburbs sounded the final death knell during the fifties, the cultural phenomenon of the American soda jerk and fountain had all but expired. Only fond memories of sweet sodas and smooth milkshakes—and the legacy of the greatest of all American creations, the soft drink—were left behind. ∎

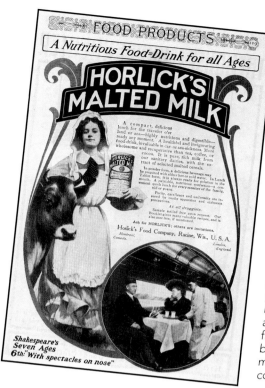

Horlick's Malted Milk
In 1886, Wisconsin dairyman William Horlick developed a new food made from whole milk, extract of wheat, and malted barley. Touted as a healthy and invigorating drink, its popularity grew rapidly. A few tablespoons mixed briskly with water turned an ordinary glass into a liquid lunch, packed with instant nutrition. Innovative soda jerks gradually added milk, ice cream, and flavored syrups to the beverage, transforming the malted milk into a new fountain concoction.

Chocolate Milkshake
"Shake, rattle, and roll"—the words of this popular song certainly describe the methods used by early milkshake pioneers as they attempted to create that perfect shake without the aid of electric mixers. In 1920, a single-spindled blender manufactured by Hamilton Beach entered the arsenal of soda fountain tools. Now, the true nature of the shake could be experienced. As tiny blades whizzed and whirled—gently aerating the mixture—a new blend was born. It was thick, rich, and smoother than any of its predecessors. Preziosi Postcards

Syrup Dispenser Progression
The evolution of the drugstore soda-fountain dispenser: from ceramic (center), to hand-drawn (right), to automatic (left). The beautiful porcelain fountain urn could be earned with a 35-gallon order of syrup, along with other premiums such as advertising clocks, prescription scales, and showcases. Courtesy of The Coca-Cola Company

continued from page 14

the installments on their vehicles. The every day rigors of life and the quest to make a living dominated the existence of the majority who owned and cherished an automobile.

Traveling great distances from their homes to do industrial work, a multitude of laborers was forced to consume meals far from the conveniences of home. Although lunch pails and sacks packed by the wife provided the noontime meal for many factory laborers, there were times when this practice born of school days proved impractical—not to mention boring. Isolated from the comforts of home with nothing but their vehicle for comfort, workers longed for a place where they could down a quick, inexpensive lunch with all the trimmings of hearth and home.

To fill the need, the "beanery" and other so-called "greasy spoons" appeared to serve the daily worker. Located in proximity to factories and in concentrated places of commerce, they became the first step in supplying food

to the average Joe. Though not in the least bit reminiscent of home, they captured the ready audience with quickness, convenience, and fair prices.

Similar variations opened in big cities to serve the growing influx of commuters, shoppers, and employees arriving around the clock. It wasn't long before a panoply of coffee-shops, lunch counters, diners, cafeterias, taverns, luncheonettes, and other eateries began to fill the streets with the smell of bacon, eggs, and hot coffee. America's restaurant boom was on! In the two decades following 1910, the estimated number of dining spots exhibited an increase of almost forty percent.

The new restaurants continued to ignore the specific needs of car customers, however. Methods that could easily be adopted to serve vehicles efficiently were neither tried nor remembered. After all, Fortune's drugstore in downtown Memphis had been serving curbside customers within their carriages as early as the turn of the century. A crew of waiters delivered soda delights directly to the customers in the street! Yet, for some reason, the bulk of businesses along America's Main Streets chose to regard this service as an oddity. Efforts were concentrated in the various formats used for inside dining. To purchase a fast meal or drink, patrons would simply have to park their cars and walk inside a building to be served.

The problem: Owners of automobiles were growing accustomed to the speed and comforts of internal-combustion living. An increasing dissatisfaction with available restaurants and their supposed conveniences was growing. For those used to the wide open spaces of the road, city cafeterias were the worst. Endless lines had to be negotiated to select food; confining quarters and the habits of others had to be tolerated while waiting. Hand-carried trays were a standard, toted individually to a spot at a communal table. Packed from elbow to elbow with unmannered gourmands, lingering was frowned

Root Beer Stand
Root beer barrel roadside stand selling "toasted" sandwiches. Circa 1920. Culver Pictures

upon. But who would want to? Oblivious to the genteel sensibilities of others, fellow diners reduced mealtime to an unenjoyable experience. Vehicle owners accustomed to the comfort of their automobiles' seats bristled at the hurried atmosphere.

While the roadside lunch wagon allowed easier access with a more forgiving parking arrangement, patrons still had to forsake the seclusion of their conveyances to place an order. Once again, the cherished motorcar had to be left behind, temporarily abandoned. Even then, food would have to be consumed while standing. Those in search of sit-down succor would have to carry their victuals back to their car.

Then, it happened: Prohibition went nationwide with a constitutional amendment in 1919. With the sale of liquor officially banned, existing soda fountains, ice cream parlors, and candy shops enjoyed a sudden rise in popularity. As back-alley operators and bootleggers began to organize a clandestine network to sell liquor, non-alcoholic liquids were rediscovered for recreational relief. Ice cream sodas became the new favorite and root beer came to be known as the "national temperance drink."

At the same time, vehicle owners were discovering just how enjoyable driving and dining really were. With the freedom for consuming alcohol disallowed, Americans held dear the remaining liberties they still had, including the pleasures of the motorcoach. By 1920, there were 8 million cars jamming the roadways with recreational eating the newest kick. Comfortable seats, glove compartments, and other accoutrements joined roll-up windows, rear-view mirrors, and windshield wipers as standard equipment. The course was set for the automobile to become as comfortable, if not more so, than the suburban dining chamber of home. With the spartan era of the Model T in decline, the environment for taking meals on wheels was primed with excitement. "Ain't we

continued on page 24

Teapot Ice Cream Cone Stand
Los Angeles ice cream stand borrowing the shape of a teapot for its attention-getting architecture. Circa 1930. Culver Pictures

Betty's Shack With Coca-Cola Signs
Below, Betty's Shack in Texas was a typical example of the roadside business trying to attract the attention of the thirsty motorist in the early decades of this century. Coca-Cola, Dr Pepper, Royal Crown Cola, and even Seven-Up were available to wash down steaks and a quick lunch. From the collections of the Texas/ Dallas History and Archives Division, Dallas Public Library

IMMORAL SODAS TO SUNDAES

America's first ice cream soda fizzed to life in October of 1874. At the time, Robert Green was working as a soda fountain concessionaire at the Franklin Institute's exhibit in Philadelphia. Serving drinks from a three-foot square dispenser, he ran out of cream for a popular beverage. Plopping a large dollop of ice cream into a flagon of flavored seltzer, he created the ice cream soda.

After sneaking a tentative sip, Green was wowed. The resulting blend of soda, syrup, and frozen cream was delightful! Without hesitation, the innocent libation was added to the menu, and by the end of the exhibition, customers showed approval by cracking their money purse. Green was taking in over $600 dollars a day in ice cream soda sales alone.

As more and more customers sampled the creamy texture of the new drink, word of the frosty frappé spread among the locals—then to surrounding states. The phenomenon spread quickly and soon ice cream sodas were slurped in fountains from New York to California.

After two decades of unbridled consumption, a placated populace began to recognize Green's handiwork as "the national beverage." As the soda addiction took root, pious Midwestern clergymen were quick to observe that the lascivious consumption was becoming uncontrollable. Not only were some Americans practicing gluttony during the week, they were now neglecting the Sabbath day of worship. The hedonistic act of sipping what was soon referred to as "the immoral soda" became a pleasurable substitute.

It wasn't long before pulpits became platforms for heated sermons. Men of the cloth rallied against the loathsome drink and denounced the country's twisted devotion to the dogma of the ice cream parlour. God-fearing congregations took heed of the warnings, and before long, a throng of righteous citizens initiated a campaign to outlaw sales of the corrupt concoction.

The Ice Cream Sundae
By the 1920s, ice cream became the fastest growing industry in America. Hailed as "America's typical food," it was consumed at the annual rate of nine quarts per person. What's more, consumer's wanted their vanilla coated in chocolate! This desire for chocolate was instrumental in lifting the cocoa-dependent economy of Ecuador out of depression. That is, until America's own Depression made those nickels to buy ice cream harder to come by. Fred D. Jordan, Unicorn Stock Photos

During the 1890s, Evanston, Illinois, became the first principality to enact laws against the "Sunday Soda Menace." Two Rivers, Wisconsin, followed with their own legislation, and soon, the banning of Sunday ice cream sodas spread nationwide. Liberated Americans, who had finally discovered a legal substitute for alcohol, became the target of a new prohibition. To the disbelief of many, a simple mixture of carbonated water and ice cream entered illegal domain.

Incensed at the excommunication of one of the best products the confection business had, fountain proprietors began searching for the ice cream soda's savior. Another "forbidden treat" had to be found, one that would legally circumvent the Sunday blue laws.

The most believable account credits fountain owner Ed Berner of Two Rivers with the unassuming creation of the new dessert. As the story goes, George Hallauer came in for a dish of ice cream and desired chocolate syrup be poured over it. Berner sampled it himself, liked it, and began to sell "ice cream with syrup" for the same price as a regular dish.

After customers began demanding it, George Giffy was forced to sell the nickel a dish treat at his soda bar in nearby Manitowoc. Afraid he was losing money on the combination, he limited sales of "the Sunday" to the seventh day.

When Giffy realized its profitability, he started promoting the "Soda-less Soda" throughout the week. To disassociate the treat with Sunday-only sales and to satisfy the vigilant clergy, the spelling was eventually altered. While the ice cream soda was not entirely forgotten, Americans now had a new Sundae. ■

Sipping Soda
This scene from the movie The Sophomore *depicts the ideal way to sip an ice cream soda: using two straws while gazing into each others eyes. Aaaaaah, what could be sweeter?* Museum of Modern Art/Film Stills Archive

Walgreen Customers with Soda
Left, a Walgreen soda jerk combines generous supplies of whipped cream, syrup, and bubbling waters to create that frozen delight—the ice cream soda! Hedrich-Blessing photograph. Courtesy the Chicago Historical Society

THOSE DACHSHUND DOGS IN A BUN

Almost nine centuries before the birth of Christ, the Greek poet Homer made reference to the roasting of sausages in his epic writings. The Romans acquired a penchant for them, too, gorging their stomachs to the limit at bawdy parties. It wasn't long before Christians denounced the cased meat as lascivious, eventually influencing the emperor Constantine to ban them from his empire.

By the time the Middle Ages were in full swing and the population a bit more tolerant of new foods, minced meat packed within intestinal wrapping lost most of its pagan mystique. Suddenly, every butcher in Europe handy with a meat grinder and a carving knife was experimenting with, and eating, sausages.

Residents of Germany's Frankfurt am Main liked their "frankfurters" ground particularly coarse, with an ample amount of seasonings added to flavor the meats. In nearby Austria, the good people of Wien (or Vienna) preferred "wieners" of a much finer consistency, easy on the spices. But, regardless of the ingredient mixture or the name, both European localities served their sausages on a plate, accompanied by a healthy helping of sauerkraut or potato salad.

When German Charles Feltman immigrated to the United States, he unknowingly brought with him the essence of this legacy, one that would eventually propel him to local fame and fortune. But like everyone else who is raised with something familiar and eventually takes it for granted, he suppressed his appetite for sausage and settled for pushing a pie wagon up and down the beach at New York's Coney Island. It was a decent living, albeit a little discouraging: customers were always inquiring whether or not he had any hot sandwiches for sale.

Convinced that sandwich vending would entail an unmanageable amount of cooking and cutting, he resisted the requests until a hot dog popped into his imagination one day in 1867. In a flash of brilliance, remembrances of Old World eating habits assembled themselves into a radically new plan for seaside profits.

It was all too simple! He would keep a small pot of warmed sausages steaming in his pushcart and sell them to the persistent customers. Sliced milk rolls would provide the means to hold the heated links, enabling spur-of-the-moment diners to enjoy their quick lunches while standing up. Unlike some of the other restaurants opening nearby, table and chair arrangements wouldn't be required, making his service almost instantaneous, cleanup non-existent.

Excited with the possibilities, Feltman approached a local wheelright named Donovan and asked if he could fashion a small burner for his food cart. Donovan accepted the task, and soon a small pot heated with coals became the core of a Feltman's new enterprise. Two at a time, he began selling his tubular lunch to curious Coney Island visitors. Everyone loved the convenience, allowing him to expand his business beyond his wildest expectations. By the time sports cartoonist T. A. Dorgan coined the term "hot dog" in 1901, Feltman managed to parlay the meager pushcart operation into a full-scale restaurant, with 1,200 waiters.

Today, the hot dog persists as the last linchpin in the regional merry-go-round of American fast food. Dictated by local tastes, hot dogs are still prepared with limitless variety. And why not? Loved and eaten across all social classes, the unheralded frankfurter has jumped the chasm from ordinary fast food to culinary common denominator. ∎

French's
Mustard Cream Salad
Francis French created the nation's largest mustard company with the development of a new formula that was light and creamy, and marketed as French's Cream Salad in this 1926 ad. Courtesy Reckitt and Coleman, Inc.

Easy Hot Dogs & Beer
What better combination than an easy hot dog and a beer, as advertised by this derelict drive-in sign near San Antonio, Texas? Great for stationary dining, but not so good when the time calls for motoring.

Hot Dog Heaven
In 1913, it was a widely held folk belief that hot dogs actually had dog meat in them. The Coney Island Chamber of Commerce banned the use of the term "hot dog" on any signs or menus. Instead, they referred to the popular boardwalk wieners as "Coney Islands!" ©1994 Michael Karl Witzel

Hot Dogs and World's Largest Drive-In
Nathan Handwerker worked slicing rolls at one of Charles Feltman's grills at Coney Island, New York. He saved $300 and leased the corner of a building on Surf Avenue in 1916. Undercutting Feltman's price, he began selling what were now being referred to as hot dogs (cartoonist T. A. Dorgan coined the term in 1901) for a nickel apiece. When the subway reached Coney Island, "Nathan's" continued to grow and became the largest hot dog emporium in the world. For the World's Largest Drive-In, the hot dog provided a potent symbol for advertising. Preziosi Postcards

Dallas Pig Stand Number 2
A short while after the first Pig Stand was opened on Chalk Hill Road (the old Dallas-Fort Worth Highway) in 1921, J. G. Kirby and R. W. Jackson constructed a second stand in Dallas. Located on Zangs Boulevard, it followed the same design philosophy as the first: close proximity to the curbside, with "carhops" servicing the arriving automobiles. Courtesy of Texas Pig Stands, Inc.

"People with cars are so lazy they don't want to get out of them to eat!"
—Jessie G. Kirby, Pig Stand founder

continued from page 19

got fun" became more than the lingo of the speakeasy, but the battle cry for the motorist as well.

Unfortunately, the simple connection between serving food to passengers within an automobile—though blatantly evident—remained to be made. Out along the expanding byways, the most hospitable sort of restaurant any traveler could hope to find was of the tea-room genre. Playing on the themes of home, these nostalgic eateries occupied buildings of historical character—namely old barns, grist mills, and vintage homes. Home-cooked meals were the specialty and alcohol never mentioned. A fair number were constructed along well-traveled tourist routes in New England, but eventually fell out of favor due to competition and amateurish management. (In the years to follow, slick operator Howard Johnson upgraded the tearoom concept with sound business practices and a visible image.)

For the time being, the most convenient choice for food pointed to the numerous "hot dog kennels" that proliferated along the motorways. At the time, anyone with a gimmick, frontage on a busy roadway, and enough scrap lumber to construct a shack could be in business. Attracting customers with a prodigious display of hand-painted signs, they capitalized on the hapless motorist "just passing through" and often became a legitimate outlet for Aunt Martha to sell her home-made sausages or Uncle Jed his hand-cranked ice cream. Despite the problems associated with quality and sanitation, reputable home-grown operations prospered.

Along with billboards and other signs, food and refreshment stand operators began to employ architecture itself to attract those passing. Bizarre constructions soon mimicked an eclectic assortment of animals and objects. Echoing the products they sold, many "programmatic" structures were erected along the established roadways during the twenties. Giant milk bottle buildings hawked malteds and three-story ice cream freezers promoted frozen desserts; oversized cranberry bottles became outlets for juice, while house-sized swines sold barbecued ribs.

Instead of using fantastic imagery as his hook, Dallas candy and tobacco magnate Jessie G. Kirby decided to exploit the habits of the average vehicle owner. "People with cars are so lazy they don't want to get out of them to eat!" was the sentiment he expressed to future partner Reuben W. Jackson when pitching the idea for a drive-by sandwich business. He believed that the time was right for an eatery geared specifically towards serving diners within their cars. A well-known Dallas physician, Jackson didn't know much about the food business but did understand the appeal of the motorcar. He was duly impressed with Kirby's practical idea of serving cars at

the curb and wasted no time providing the initial $10,000 financing needed for a corporation that would construct a prototype pork stand.

In the fall of 1921, the American automobile and the restaurant collided head on, forever altering the nature of dining along the roadways. That year, Kirby and Jackson's ambitious food enterprise dubbed the "Pig Stand" began offering its tasty sandwiches to the motorists of Texas, enticing automotive commuters to exit their speeding path on the bustling Dallas-Fort Worth Highway to "Eat a Pig Sandwich." One by one, car customers hungry for something new eased off the throttle to become part of the festive grand opening. On the busy cross street bordering the Pig Stand's lot, an assortment of motor vehicles awaited their turn in line.

Curiously enough, the scene was more reminiscent of a curbside traffic jam than a restaurant opening. But the problems of traffic

The Claude Neon Pig
Over seventy years old, the famous Pig Sandwich sign manufactured by the Claude Federal Neon Company still delights customers. Four additional pig signs remain, and owner Richard Hailey plans to display them at other Pig Stand locations. When an infringement lawsuit against the Hard Rock Cafe (a Pig Sandwich appeared on the their menu) went to court in the early 1990s, Hailey wheeled the large sign into the courtroom as evidence. Judgment for the plaintiff: the "Pig Sandwich" belongs exclusively to the Pig Stands restaurants! Broadway location dining room, San Antonio, Texas

Royce Hailey and the Carhops
On the bottom row, fourth from the left is Royce Hailey, the carhop who started with the Pig Stands on February 15, 1930. He worked his way up through the organization doing every job imaginable and ultimately became the president of the company in 1955. Today, his son, Richard Hailey, continues the Pig Stand tradition. This Pig Stand was located on East Grand in Dallas, Texas. Courtesy of Texas Pig Stands, Inc.

control proved minimal: automobilists savvy to the latest fads picked right up on the concept. Attracted by the economical prices, Tin Lizzy owners comprised the majority of the first customers, with operators of refined vehicles such as the Packard Twin Six and the Cadillac Touring Sedan eventually vying for space at the junction.

As the first month of operation drew to a close, local residents and passing travelers were discovering for themselves the thrill of eating in your car. Rewarded within the privacy of their vehicles with savory pork sandwiches, bottled soda beverages, and courteous service, there were no surprises or disappointments. No longer would the casual motorist have to leave the privacy of his or her vehicle to suffer the perceived indignities of the typical roadside food operation. The family picnic could now be had within the motorcar itself,

effectively converting any automobile into a dining room on wheels. At long last, America had its "new motor lunch."

As both the famished and curious steered in for service, dapper young men accosted the speeding vehicles during their final moments of deceleration. Wasting no time with formalities, they jumped without hesitation right up onto machines moving along the curbside to gather food orders. Fortunately, most automotive models were equipped with running boards in those days: side-mounted strips of metal running under the length of each side door. Normally, these platforms were used by the driver or passenger to facilitate safe entry. When unused as a step, they held spare tires or the occasional suitcase.

To the lunchers' delight, the daring young servers of the Texas Pig Stands superseded both of these mundane applications. As customers became acquainted with the idea of waiters jumping up on their cars, many began to wonder if the thin sideboards had been designed just for them! In an age of idols and ballyhoo typified by pole-sitters and daredevils, it was just the type of brash exhibitionism needed to attract public interest and a write-up in the local newspaper.

In reality, the motivation was more basic for the jumping order takers: Those who got to the car first were the ones who made the best tips. Therefore, speed was of the utmost importance. By the time an automobile braked to a complete stop, one of the competitive curb boys would be hanging off its side, his

continued to page 30

Pig Stand Menu
The breakfast menu from the Number 2 stand, circa 1930.
Courtesy Chuck Sturm

PIG STANDS, INC.

Good Morning!

We respectfully suggest to You any one of these appetizing . . .

CLUB BREAKFASTS

No. 1
One Egg, Ham, Bacon or Brookfield Sausage, Toast, Jelly and Coffee
25c

No. 2
Half Grapefruit, One Egg, Ham, Bacon or Brookfield Sausage, Toast, Jelly and Coffee
35c

No. 3
Half Grapefruit, Two Eggs, Toast Jelly and Coffee
35c

No. 4
Cereal with Cream, Two Eggs, Ham Bacon or Brookfield Sausage, Toast Jelly, Coffee
45c

Our Eggs Are Scrambled in Pure Cream and Fried in Butter

PIG STANDS, INC.

Or . . .

if You prefer for Breakfast . . .

Orange Juice	.10
Tomato Juice	.10
Pineapple Juice	.10
Grapefruit Juice	.10
Half Grapefruit	.10
Ham and Eggs, Toast, Jelly and Coffee	.30
Bacon and Eggs, Toast, Jelly and Coffee	.30
Brookfield Sausage and Eggs, Toast Jelly and Coffee	.30
Ham or Bacon Omelette, Toast Jelly and Coffee	.35
Two Eggs, any style, Toast, Jelly and Coffee	.25
Plain Omelette, Toast, Jelly and Coffee	.25
One Egg, Toast, Jelly and Coffee	.20
Hot Cakes, Melted Butter and Maple Syrup	.15
Side Order of Ham, Bacon or Brookfield Sausage	.15
Cereals with Cream	.15

PIG STANDS, PIG STANDS, EVERYWHERE

Pioneering the Drive-Thru Window
The drive-thru window was an idea tried in 1931 at the California Pig Stand Number 21. Customers could drive-in, place their order, and exit. It was quick and convenient, the basic model for the way fast-food businesses operate today. The only difference was that the order taker was not a machine.
Courtesy of Texas Pig Stands, Inc.

Crowd Loves Pig Stand Number 21
After California Pig Stand Number 21 was remodeled, crowds charged with Golden Bear Coffee posed happily for a photograph. Circa mid-1930s. Courtesy of Texas Pig Stands, Inc.

Royce Hailey With Pig Sign
Coca-Cola and the Pig Sandwich—a winning combination for Royce Hailey, ex-carhop turned chain owner. Today, son Richard Hailey continues the tradition of the sliced pork lunch and has taken over the reins from his dad. From the collections of the Texas/Dallas History and Archives Division, Dallas Public Library

Octagonal Los Angeles Stand
By 1930, more operators were entering the market with their own food stands. Basic Pig Stand designs were upgraded with colored tile and new signboards. But even those were not enough: a large "Sandwiches" sign lettered in neon now occupied a place of prominence, almost as large as the stand itself! Courtesy of Texas Pig Stands, Inc.

Beaumont Circular Pig Stand
Beaumont was the Texas town where Royce Hailey came up with his most famous invention: Texas Toast. Around 1941, he was working as the district manager and began experimenting with bread. One day, he asked the Rainbo Bakery to slice his loaves thicker and was presented with slabs that were simply too big to fit in the toaster. One of the cooks suggested that they butter them and toast both sides on the grill. It was a good idea: they turned out extremely moist with a flavor totally different from regular toast. Another cook suggested they call it "Texas Toast" and the rest is history. Unfortunately, Hailey failed to patent the invention. This circular Pig Stand was located on Calder Avenue. Circa 1941. Courtesy of Texas Pig Stands, Inc.

San Antonio Streamline Pig Stand
By 1939, the outdated buildings typical of the early locations was retired. Streamlined traffic-stoppers like this impressive San Antonio tower unit took the barbecued pork sandwich to a new level. Courtesy of Texas Pig Stands, Inc.

Broadway Pig Stand
The Texas Pig Stands are still alive and well and thriving in the Lone Star State. The Broadway location in San Antonio is reported to be one of the nation's oldest sit-down restaurants. San Antonio, Texas

A&W Stand
In 1921, the nation's first A&W Root Beer stand opened on the corner of K and 19th Streets in Sacramento. Pioneering fast-food franchising much like the Singer Company sold its sewing machines, A&W allowed investors to sell its popular refreshment products. After Mr. Wright's half of the partnership was bought out by Allen in 1924, a major push to franchise the root beer was undertaken. Color schemes were duplicated, along with architecture, signs, and trademarks. Allen's biggest transaction followed in 1927 when young J. Willard Marriott purchased the rights to sell the A&W brand in the Washington, D. C. market. Eventually, his fledgling hole-in-the-wall stand grew into the Hot Shoppes drive-in chain. A&W Restaurants, Inc.

A&W Root Beer Barrel Stand
Right, what better way to entice customers to purchase root beer than to construct a building like a giant root beer barrel? It was a concept that worked for many franchisees of the A&W brew during the twenties and thirties and continued well into the 1950s. A&W Restaurants, Inc.

continued from page 27
face peering through the driver's side window. As fast as the operator behind the steering wheel could rattle off his or her order, the energetic order taker would be gone. With all the energy of youth, the boys snapped up food requests as fast as humanly possible. Leaping on and off the shifting line of auto

platforms with a practiced style, they dodged crazily between a dozen or more sputtering vehicles and were gone.

As the curb filled up, they ran back and forth to the small board-and-batten box that housed the kitchen, delivering their requests to the short-order man working his craft within the wooden structure. As the orders came up, efficient servers scooped up the entrees with one hand and snatched up a couple of frosty Coca-Cola bottles with the other. Sprinting a return to the ordering vehicle with food in hand, they were greeted by the vehicle occupants with child-like anticipation. As paper-wrapped meals were thrust through the customer's side window, coins and greenbacks were exchanged. Lightning speed and friendliness were rewarded generously by the mobile visitors; a bulging pocket full of tips was the only ballast that slowed the frenetic pace.

The nation's first automotive food servers quickly became a local phenomenon and the term "carhop" was coined to describe the flashy combination of waiter, busboy, cashier, and daredevil. Soon, other operations picked up on the style. It wasn't long before the carhopping carboy of the Pig Stand pushed out the saddle-jumping cowboy of the rodeo as the new hero of the American West. As news of the new serving style spread beyond the expanse of Texas, motorists lauded the motoring waiter as just another benefit of automobile ownership. After all, the gasoline station had its service attendant and the lubritorium its grease monkey. Why should the roadside food stand be any different?

A number of operators were answering that question with their own car service, including those on the West Coast. Around the same time Kirby's car servers were thrilling Dallas customers, Roy W. Allen was training his own crew of "tray-boys" to work at his drive-in root beer stand in California. According to a May 1968 article in *Drive-In Restaurant*, it all started in 1918:

Roy W. Allen met a traveling chemist who boasted of a special formula he had concocted for draft root beer and explained how well it would sell for a nickel a glass. Allen was skeptical, but tried the drink anyway. That sip proved to be worth a fortune.

Mr. Allen was going about his business of purchasing old hotels and restaurants to re-model for resale when at one establishment in Flagstaff, Arizona, Allen met a traveling chemist who boasted of a special formula he had concocted for draft root beer. Raving about this brew's taste, he urged Allen to serve the frothy drink at the hotel and explained how well it would sell for a nickel a glass. Allen was skeptical, but tried the drink anyway. That first sip proved to be worth a small fortune.

Without delay, an agreement was made between the two men to produce and market the root beer concentrate. Armed with the confidence afforded by the tasty formula, Allen opened a small root beer stand in the small town of Lodi, California, and began selling icy refreshments to the public on a busy corner downtown. By the end of 1919, his

foaming beverage made from a secret mixture of herbs, spices, barks, and berries became a well-known thirst-quencher in the area. It was the height of Prohibition, and the small stand easily attracted an admirable volume of business. Encouraged by the success and profits of this first refreshment shack, he decided to construct a duplicate outlet in Stockton.

A&W Tray-Boys & Girls at Stand
Above, at this circa 1925 A&W stand in Salt Lake City, Utah, "tray-boys" and "tray-girls" line up with trays in hand. In the background, the heat of the day is already rising—root beer customers are on their way! A&W Restaurants, Inc.

A&W Round Stand
Left, a crude version of the streamlined drive-in structures to come, circa 1940s. Hot dogs, root beer, and popcorn were America's first automotive comfort foods. A&W Restaurants, Inc.

Forties A&W Tray-Boy With Cars
J. Willard Marriott employed the service of young men to cart what was known as "Food for the Whole Family" to motorists in cars. These "running boys" were an updated version of the car-serving prototype of the twenties, now sporting two-toned suit jacket, black tie, white shirt, and white brimmed hat. A round neon sign caught the look of the car server in full stride and soon became a beacon for those in the Washington, D. C. area. Courtesy Library of Congress

In 1920, an employee from the Lodi location, Frank Wright, officially joined the drink enterprise and the search for a new name was undertaken. Utilizing the first initials of their names—"A" for Allen and "W" for Wright—the team opted for simplicity and formally christened their temperance beverage A&W Root Beer.

With a brand identifier established, the pioneering refreshment stands (operating without a defined brand) in Stockton and Lodi were leased to other operators. The newly formed soft drink pair had more ambitious plans: an entirely different operation would be built in Sacramento, with more to follow. Featuring the delivery of frosty mugs right out to the customer, they would become California's first drive-ins.

In 1921, the nation's first root beer stand using the A&W name opened on the corner of K and 19th Streets in Sacramento. Like their Texas cousins, the peppy tray-boys (and later, tray-girls) introduced Californians to the magic of car service and developed their own unique serving style. But unlike the Pig Stand's free-wheeling acrobatics, A&W's curb service was more subdued: workers toted multiple mugs of brew atop sturdy trays within a defined parking area. Presented in a mug made of characteristically heavy glass, root beer was a refreshment that required ginger handling during delivery. Unlike bottles of soda pop that were bandied about with little care, fluted decanters had to be carried with more thought. They required retrieval to a central washing area where they were cleaned for the next batch of customers. As a result, cars weren't allowed to zip up to the curb and drive away at their own leisure. Waiting in a patient and orderly fashion was a required practice.

In the end, however, the diverse styles Roy Allen and J. G. Kirby presented to serve food and drink to patrons waiting within their automobiles were inconsequential. What mattered most was the ultimate digression from established patterns of food service had finally been initiated. Now, two major markets were experimenting with a natural symbiosis: recreational dining and the gasoline-powered automobile.

With only a minimal investment in structure and virtually none in advertising, the Pig Stands fixed the notion that customers really did like to eat inside their cars and would gladly patronize restaurants that subscribed to that mode. Similarly, the A&W Root Beer stands made a point for refreshment: Motorists speeding by in an auto would—and actually preferred to—drive in for something as simple as a cold beverage. No longer were the normal styles enough to satisfy; the bustling city cafeteria was destined to become the "carfeteria" and the cramped luncheonette a full-blown drive-in with all the room of the great outdoors.

Although both of these operations became the nation's first models for the coming glut of roadside eateries and the transition to eating-on-the-go, their potential was somewhat hampered by their adherence to established menus. While barbecue was a big favorite in many regions of the country, it was not as highly esteemed in others. Similarly, while root beer was loved in Utah, other states remained loyal to soft drinks such as Coca-Cola, Dr Pepper, or Moxie. One person's milkshake was another's malted. In an age preceding the dominant influence of national advertising, many people were slow to try new things—especially tastes that they were not accustomed to.

As a departure from what appeared to be an inevitable sequence of events, the union of barbecue sandwich and root beer drink would not become the combination to push the drive-in phenomenon into the future. A new food was required, an entree that could become nationally popular. Even then, it would have to be simple, made with readily available materials, by a variety of operators. To become a universal standard for quick dining, it would have to possess an inbred appeal that evoked, "I am the food for automotive dining." Coincidentally, there was one comestible already being flipped and fried on griddles throughout America that fit these criteria. The only qualities it lacked to become the hand-held meal of the motorist were notoriety, respect, and promotion. Something plump, juicy, and covered with sesame seeds was almost visible over the horizon. For all those who loved to eat within their automobiles and acknowledged that the future of dining along the roadways was the drive-in restaurant, the best was yet to come. ■

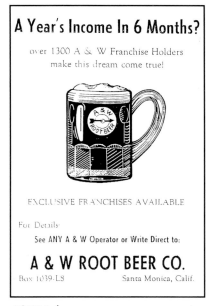

A&W Ad
A year's income in six months? How could an adventurous entrepreneur refuse? A&W ad circa 1940.

McDonald's Had Some Carhops

*"Situated across the street from Monrovia's municipal airport,
they called their stand the 'Airdrome' and began attracting motorists
upon their arrival and departure."*

The brothers McDonald left New Hampshire to avoid the fate that had befallen their father: sudden unemployment. After toiling forty-two years as a shoe factory foreman, his job was eliminated along with thousands of others working New England's cotton mills and textile plants. To escape the depressed conditions and to find their own financial independence, Richard and Maurice headed to California in search of a more promising future.

By 1928, they managed to find work in the movie business transporting sets and driving trucks for Columbia Studios. The pay was adequate and within a few years, their "careers" in show business afforded the opportunity to lease a movie theater in the town of Glendora. They renamed it the Beacon, but never managed to pack in the large crowds they had anticipated. Short of funds at the end of the month, they had no choice but to consider other alternatives.

With eyes bent to finding a money-maker, they were soon inspired by two occurrences that shaped their economic destiny. It all started when they took notice of the steady line of customers wolfing frankfurters and guzzling root beer at Walt Wiley's local refreshment shack. With little overhead and minimal stock, he was handling quite a respectable volume of clientele. After they learned that a local Sunkist packing plant was discarding perfectly good fruit, the answer to their problems began to gel: buy the fallen fruit for a steal, squeeze it into juice, and sell it along with hot dogs from a roadside food stand!

In 1937, a deal was made to purchase the oranges at twenty-dozen for a quarter. With more enthusiasm than actual restaurant experience, the McDonalds borrowed some lumber and constructed a tiny octagonal building on Huntington Drive, in nearby Arcadia. A close neighbor to Monrovia's municipal airport, they called their stand the "Airdrome" and began attracting motorists upon their arrival and departure. Being less than two miles from the Santa Anita racetrack didn't hurt, either: jockeys and horse trainers became loyal regulars. To satisfy the following, ushers were recycled from the Beacon to serve as carhops.

According to "Skeeter" Kobzeff, one of the original car girls, "everything was citrus back then…and orange juice was everywhere!" The demand was so great that they soon decided to open another stand—a separate structure— right across the street. Shaped as what Richard McDonald described as "a beautiful orange," it was manned by one lone attendant during the months of summer. In 1939, fresh-squeezed orange juice was served from the hut. Hundreds of motorists stopped in daily to be refreshed while others just stared or took snapshots. The great orange was a magnet for cars.

By this time, Mac and Maurice were devout believers of drive-in dining. They obtained financing for a larger operation and by 1940, sold the juice stand and closed down their airport unit. After finding a promising location in San Bernardino, they sliced the Airdrome in two pieces and had it transported to the new site at Fourteenth and E Streets. As curious students from a nearby high school watched, workmen remodeled, enlarged, then carefully reassembled the faceted building.

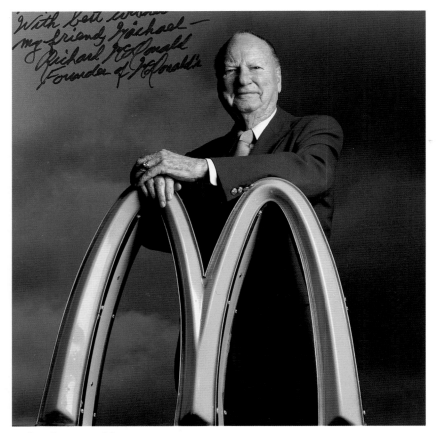

Richard McDonald Portrait
Richard and brother "Mac" Maurice McDonald were the originators of the roadside dining system now referred to as "fast food." In every sense, their story is a true Horatio Alger tale, rich with intrigue, humor, and excitement. The next time you bite into a burger, take a moment and think of the McDonalds…they started it all. ©1994 Steven Lewis

The McDonald Brothers Drive-In

In 1940, the McDonald brothers sliced their Airdrome orange juice stand in two pieces and transported it to a new site at Fourteenth and E Streets in San Bernardino, California. It was remodeled, and twenty carhops in satin uniforms hired. On weekend nights, 125 cars touched fenders in the parking lot
Courtesy Richard McDonald

Richard McDonald sketched "Speedy" as a new hamburger-faced mascot and installed a neon sign featuring the blinking chef roadside. Having a similar effect on the passing traffic as the colorful fruit stand, his engaging burger face pulled in diners with a friendly smile—the kids loved him! Twenty carhops in satin uniforms handled the onslaught to come: on weekend nights, 125 cars touched fenders in the parking lot! By 1948, revenues from the wonder topped $200,000. Mac and Maurice had their plates piled with American dream.

Despite the success, the McDonald brothers grew restless. After World War II, they could sense customers were becoming impatient with the service and speed of the hops. Invisible to the layman, the "faults" in their operation were growing evident. Shortly, they would decide to close the drive-in, fire the carhops, cool the barbecue pit, dump the silverware, and reduce the menu. America's prototype of the fast-food stand that served "hamburgers, Cokes, and French fries" was on its way. ∎

MILDRED "SKEETER" KOBZEFF, THE AIRDROME

In 1937, Richard and Maurice McDonald opened the Airdrome in Arcadia, California. At the time, they also managed the Beacon Theater in Glendora and recruited the usherettes for car service. Mildred "Skeeter" Kobzeff became one of their first carhops and served auto patrons with burgers, dogs, orange juice, coffee, and beer (although Skeeter's mom didn't really approve of alcohol). During her first hours of employment, Skeeter found out that the roadside refreshment biz was more than just taking car orders: she also had to cook, cashier, and clean!

Skeeter often borrowed her parents' car to get to work and one day her father discovered a pair of men's boxer shorts lying in the backseat. He wasn't happy about the discovery and Skeeter had quite a time explaining where the mysterious underwear came from. Although she was determined to uncover the prankster, she never found out who owned them! Fortunately, the dubious incident had a happy ending: her mom washed the shorts and they eventually became part of her dad's wardrobe.

By the time the Airdrome was moved to San Bernardino and the McDonalds gained notoriety with their fast-food system, Kobzeff left the carhopping business for good. The demands of three children replaced the wants of car customers, later augmented by four grandchildren. Currently, she is regarded by the locals as the "Unofficial Glendora Historian" and participates as an active member of local clubs and historical organizations. She has been a staff writer on the *Glendoran Magazine* since it started in 1982 and still finds time in her schedule for a part-time job. ■

SEATTLE'S ROADSIDE IGLOO

*"The engaging little Eskimo that smiled upon the passing traffic
and shone its colorful palette of neon onto the roadway was silenced forever,
demolished by the thoughtless forces of change."*

When Seattle's Igloo Drive-In opened during the forties, the American roadside was still a magical place. Numerous commercial buildings typified by out-of-scale hot dogs, gigantic root beer barrels, house-sized milk bottles, colossal vegetables, and overgrown animals dotted the highways coast to coast. The increase in motoring brought on by better roads and the automobile's proliferation provided a surge of prospective customers. With a corresponding rise in advertising stimulus competing for attention, ordinary signs and billboards lost much of their impact.

Creative refreshment stand operators learned that in order to stand out among the cacophony of images, this new class of visual excitement had to be employed. Inducing motorists to pilot vehicles from the roadbed called for a hint of the spectacular. Strong symbolism and eye-popping themes employed by "programmatic" architecture proved the hook

Igloo Drive-In Menu Courtesy Ralph Grossman

required to lure those passing to stop and spend.

The whimsical appeal of these mimetic styles proved to be what Ralph Grossman and Ernie Hughes were looking for when planning their proposed Seattle drive-in. With a long list of prospective building designs ruled out by both as "ordinary," Hughes suggested the eatery be shaped in the form of an igloo. Acknowledged by both as a stroke of genius, the partners soon raised the extra capital required to commence construction. On what seemed like an appropriate date to begin work on a building planning to masquerade, construction crews broke ground on Halloween day, 1940.

Enticed by the promise of generous tips and salary, Seattle's most attractive girls were persuaded to try their luck as tray-girls. A bevy of beautiful women clad in abbreviated skirts and high boots proved to be the perfect magnet to interrupt the flow of traffic on Denny Way. Aggressively recruited from the pool of underpaid usherettes employed at local movie theaters, the majority welcomed the change to serving car customers. Wages were better and they could become part of the real-life movie as seen through the motorists' windshield.

Every night, a new featurette played out in the Igloo's parking lot. Music piped to speakers provided the opening soundtrack for the production, as bright spotlights illuminated the domes. Directed by the commotion to drive on in, cars of all makes and models lined up for a front row seat. Right on cue, food orders were delivered in perfect time. Carhops had the right moves and the right lines.

A close-up revealed young lovers of the day enjoying fast food and passionate kisses in the front seat. Dissolving to the rear bench, youngsters were showcased slurping up milkshakes, a drip-drop lost here and there. Panning left, a cameo from mom and dad…married couples renewing vows over a double-malted and sack of onion rings. Zooming in on a serving tray attached to a car window, deluxe cheeseburgers could be seen stacked high with all the trimmings. Wonderful sights, sounds, and smells—all part of the Igloo's script, written specifically for the customer's satisfaction.

Unfortunately, the Igloo's sparkling domes ended up being cut from the closing reel. Years ago, their final fate was sealed by the business of economics and perceived aesthetics. In the quest for profits, they succumbed swiftly to the wrecker's ball with nary a complaint from the public. The engaging little Eskimo that smiled upon the passing traffic and shone its colorful palette of neon onto the roadway was silenced forever, demolished by the thoughtless forces of change.

Revamped, regraded, resurfaced, and ultimately resold, the small patch of land once bustling with short-skirted carhops, chromed automobiles, and hamburger-hungry motorists was redesignated for more significant usage. Within a few years, an uncontrolled glut of franchised burger factories took up

Igloo Tetons

Seattle's Igloo Drive-In was a well-known attraction during the 1940s. Inside seating for seventy customers made the dual-domed wonder attractive to those who occasionally liked to eat in a dining room. Outside, wintertime carhops wore ski-togs from Nordstrom with high white boots; in summertime, they *sported short skirts. Owners Ralph Grossman and Ernie Hughes recruited most of the good-looking girls from local theaters to work as carhops. Ralph and Ernie also had the same taste in convertibles. Like their twin-domed Igloo Drive-In, they liked their automobiles to match. Courtesy Ralph Grossman*

positions all over Seattle. The days of Ralph and Ernie's grilled "Husky Burgers" and ice-cold "Boeing Bombers" had ended abruptly. Progress, in the form of an automobile repair shop catering to motor vehicles imported from overseas, had usurped the Igloo's rightful place along the American roadside. ∎

BLACKIE'S DRIVE-IN IS RELISHED

"Nel Flavin still makes hot-pepper relish the same way she did when Blackie's first opened—and customers can still have as much as they like on their hot dogs!"

As the sun falls below the tree line and the sky floods with the sienna hues of dusk, Blackie's Drive-In begins an incredible transformation. At just the right moment, a bank of switches are flipped from within. Electrical impulses race through wiring and into transformer coils, energizing electrodes designed to stimulate rare gases trapped within glass tubing.

Milliseconds later, the red-hot outline of the rooftop marquee momentarily blinks, then stabilizes, branding an indelible image into the darkness. In accompaniment to the neon buzz, colorful crests mounted at each side of the structure flash to life, proclaiming its glory to the night. No golden arch can match the effect, nor passing car resist the sight.

Drawn from the roadbed to this light-filled oasis, a continuous flow of traffic pours into the warm circle of light bathing the parking lot. Families, singles, seniors, and truck drivers—anyone and everyone enters through the open breezeway with one thing on their mind: a piping hot tubesteak topped with the delicious home-made relish that has made Blackie's a local legend. Comfortably perched upon the row of counter stools chomping their dogs,

customers tentatively exchange glances—then smiles of approval as depleted containers are refilled with the popular mash.

Not a word is spoken as utensils are thrust into the mix from all directions, copious amounts of zesty condiment spooned up and ingested. At Blackie's, there's no time for idle talk or pleasantries; the obsessive hunger for a home-style frankfurter smothered in hot-pepper relish reigns as the unabashed ruler of all thought and action. This singularity of mind is plainly echoed by the limited food menu and abbreviated ordering language customers use to make their food requests. In contrast with the soda jerk or lunch counter waitress of yesteryear (who developed their own jargon to facilitate quick orders), the accepted syntax at Blackie's calls for simplified, one-word commands. Protocol dictates that diners desiring a hot dog call out their order directly to the counter girl, where it's rebroadcast verbatim to the cook in charge of assembling franks.

Experienced alumni properly schooled in Blackie's succinct ordering vocabulary call out "one, two, or three," depending on their appetite and ability to digest large amounts of peppers. Since first timers invariably make requests with complete sentences, it's easy to distinguish the neophyte from a regular! Regardless of the method used, drive-in car customers make it clear by the shear quantities consumed that the enticing flavor of Blackie's homemade relish is what cements their loyalty to this established roadside eatery.

To this day, owner Nel Flavin persists in maintaining that customer devotion, insisting that the flavorful concoction responsible for the success be made from scratch. Ensuring that the secret family recipe used for the past sixty-five years is still followed religiously, she fiercely defends all attempts to downgrade the quality of her ingredients. She still makes the relish the same way she did when Blackie's first opened—and customers can still have as much as they like on their hot dogs!

In the creative atmosphere of her kitchen, ordinary pots and pans take on the identity of artisan's tools. Fresh-from-the-farm vegetables and a palette of natural spices become her medium. In her grasp, a wooden cooking spoon becomes a precision utensil. Her stove serves as the easel on which she works her special cookery. Like an Old World master, she becomes lost in her craft, chopping, dicing, slicing—transforming otherwise unexceptional ingredients into a culinary labor of love.

Ultimately, when her refined mixture is ladled upon the cylindrical canvas of a steaming dog and bun, the combination becomes a new entity. Existing in the temporal realm of what the eye can see and nose can smell momentarily, Flavin's hot-pepper relish makes the final transition to personal memory by way of the tastebuds. There, it becomes edible art. For the devotees eager to take a taste of what the real roadside has to offer, Blackie's Drive-In will always be a true masterpiece of pleasurable roadside dining. ■

Blackie's Marquee
Mounted on each of Blackie's dual octagonal towers, multi-colored crests illuminate the parking lot during the evening hours.

Blackie's Drive-In

Blackie's still serves up hot dogs with homemade relish to motoring customers. It's tucked away in Cheshire, Connecticut—off the beaten path and a welcome find for the hungry traveler not afraid of leaving the interstate. Taking the architectural cues from the food stands that proliferated in California during the thirties, Blackie's features two octagonal structures. At the center, a double-door garage setup opens to welcome customers.

FROM PAPER BAGS TO WINDOW TRAYS

When the first drive-in restaurants began serving customers in their automobiles during the twenties, it was novelty enough just to have food delivered by carhop. At most operations, sandwiches were simply wrapped in waxed paper and drinks served out of the bottle. Car servers clutched entrees in their hands and delivered large food orders with the aid of paper sacks.

As the number of eateries featuring car service multiplied, simply tossing a barbecue sandwich through an open car window became unacceptable. While car customers loved the independent ambiance afforded by the new gimmick of in-car dining, they didn't discourage improvements in the areas of added convenience and service. All attempts to further civilize the drive-in dining procedure were welcomed.

Taking their cues from interior "sit-down" restaurants and their waitresses, drive-in eateries adopted standard serving trays for parking lot use. After a short stint in customers' laps, they were upgraded for automotive service by the simple addition of window clips permanently attached to one side. Before long, an extended support leg was grafted onto the tray's underside, allowing larger food orders—complete with heavy serving china, silverware, and glasses—to be safely balanced carside.

With the window-mounted serving tray an accepted accessory of the carhop, the pleasure of eating within an automobile increased dramatically. Food and beverages were now at arm's length, and the chance for accidental spillage within the passenger compartment reduced. Best of all, when the meal was finished, greasy dishes and napkins could be removed from the car and placed on the exterior platform. Carhops would bus the load, trash the garbage, and pocket the pile of change left beneath.

Of course, the use of car trays had its share of drawbacks during periods of inclement weather. Wind caused many of the flats to become airborne, resulting in a sticky mess of flipped-over food. When it rained, trays became impromptu catch-basins for water, reducing already-greasy French fries to a soggy mess. To allow customers the enjoyment of meals shielded from the elements, radical improvements were necessary.

Fortunately, the drive-in industry's wish list was promptly filled when companies introduced a new line of platforms. Available in a range of sizes, models like the "TraCo" number 26 were

TraCo Serving Trays
Serving trays were not confined to the outside of the vehicle. Many models were available to clip to the steering wheel or occupy the space in front of the passenger.

For
DRIVE-IN SERVICE

SERV-A-CAR
Trays and Accessories

*W*ith the window-mounted serving tray an accepted accessory of the carhop, the pleasure of eating within an automobile increased dramatically. When the meal was finished, greasy dishes and napkins could be removed from the car and placed on the exterior platform.

Trays Available In Two Sizes - No. 300 Standard 10" x 14" and No. 500 Large 12" x 17".

No. A 100 Napkin & Straw Holder. Attaches instantly to the side of either tray. For tray or counter use.

No. A 200 Ice Cream Cup Holder. Holds up to 6 cups. May be used in conjunction with either tray or individually.

Go Modern...

• SEE YOUR DEALER OR WRITE FOR FULL INFORMATION •

Serv-A-Car Trays and Accessories
Serving trays came in all shapes and sizes. Wire-rack types were all the rage for some time, complete with special holders that organized napkins, salt and pepper, and cradled multiple ice cream cones.

specifically designed for use within a car's interior. Attached to the steering wheel with two molded brackets, an extra arm hooked up to the vent window to stabilize. Another version was designed just for passengers, aided by an assembly that braced against the dash. Some were even made from wire mesh.

Henry Boos shook it all up in 1929 when he crafted a long serving board that stretched from door-to-door inside the car. He field tested the thin wooden "table" at the Roberts Brothers Drive-Ins in Los Angeles and found a receptive audience with his brother-in-law's regular customers. The interior tray unit caught on quickly, and soon, manufacturers were mass producing it.

Upgraded with pressed aluminum, two fully loaded 6 by 46 inch trays could be installed for diners in the front and backseat and adjusted to fit across virtually any car.

As drive-ins were edged out by coffee-shops, walkup fast food stands, and the drive-thru franchise, serving trays lost favor with the motorist. Waiting for a carhop to serve a meal and remove the dishes became a luxury of another era. The hand-held window clip tray, interior steering wheel mount, and long buckboard contraption were now too impractical. Once again, American motorists were content to eat their automotive meals from paper bags. ■

Carhop at Wagner's Drive-In
No bagged meal from a fast-food restaurant will ever compare with the style of service provided by the classic drive-in. Food is presented with style, hung on the window for all to see, admire…and consume. At drive-ins across America— such as Wagner's in St. Louis Park, Minnesota—this is still the way food is served today. Michael Dregni

Kings-X Drive-In Meal on a Tray

When competing hamburger outlets came to Wichita, Kansas, during the sixties, they brought with them simple menus consisting of only a few items. In contrast, the Kings-X restaurants had an elaborate selection. To reduce confusion for the customer and to allow for easier identification of food when delivered, color-coded packaging was implemented. Every burger selection had its own unique color. Courtesy Kings-X Inc.

CHAPTER TWO

THE CIRCULAR MECCA
OF NEON

Traveling fry cook Walter Anderson settled down in the heartland of America and opened up a small lunch wagon in 1916. It was a spartan affair, without the luxuries of Wichita's fancy restaurants—but it did feature a serving counter, three stools, and a flat-iron fry griddle. That simple trio was enough for An-

derson. His determination to elevate the much-maligned hamburger from its lowly position to one of prominence was more important.

By the early 1900s, the hamburger had gained a rather inauspicious reputation. Like the hot dog, the true composition of cooked burger was difficult to determine by mere

continued on page 52

White Castle Crenelated Tower
Walter Anderson teamed up with Wichita, Kansas, real estate and insurance man Edgar Waldo "Billy" Ingram in 1921 to enlarge his burger operation. With a $700 loan and a lot of optimism, Anderson constructed his fourth, and most memorable, burger emporium from rusticated concrete block. It was the beginning of the White Castle chain and the nationwide standardization of the hamburger. Today, Wichita, Kansas, is a magnet for fast-food restaurants. Courtesy of Kings-X Inc.

Bart's Drive-In
Previous pages, this circular drive-in (located in Portland, Oregon) was called Bart's during the forties and was later changed over to The Speck during the fifties. In close proximity to Franklin High School, it was a favorite destination for cruisers. Today, a Burger King operates from this location, dedicating its decor to the memory of the past tenants: metal-flake vinyl covers the seats and images of classic cars dominate the interior walls. Oregon Historical Society

BIRTHPLACE OF THE HAMBURGER

Sure, history books tell of the Tartar's fondness for raw meat and how sailors from Germany loved to order Hamburg Style Steak upon their arrival in the New World. The real question is: Who created America's first all-beef patty, ancestral prototype of today's Quarter Pounder, Big Mac, and Whopper?

Pinpointing the origination of the hamburger to one particular person has proven more difficult to substantiate than the introduction of buttered toast. From localities across the nation, a roster of colorful characters have all staked their claim to the honor, forever obscuring the faint lines of fast-food lineage.

Popular food folklore—peppered with a light sprinkling of facts—often gives the top billing to "Hamburger" Charlie Nagreen, an inventive resident of Seymour, Wisconsin. Seems it all started somewhere around 1885, when fifteen-year-old Charlie began peddling his chopped beef to the throng of hungry visitors attending the Outgamie County Fair.

Worried about soiling their hands with grease, a few genteel patrons asked if Nagreen could supply a more sanitary way of toting the snack meat. Responding with a sizzling stroke of genius, he slapped one of his cooked patties between two slices of bread—and presto! The first truly portable combination of ground beef and bread became a reality.

Five states to the south, the burger-loving denizens of Athens, Texas, have posted a plaque promoting their own history. For them, the original father of the blessed burger has been and always will be legendary lunch counter owner, operator, cook, and chief bottle washer Uncle "Fletch" Davis.

By the latter part of the 1890s, old Dave gained a notable reputation locally for his fried patties of steer. He decorated his first hand-held version with a healthy dose of hot mustard, crowned it with a slice of Bermuda onion, and nestled the stackup between dual slabs of home-made bread. *Voilà,* pardner—the hamburger was born!

The state of Ohio throws its own entry onto the griddle with the exploits of Akronite Frank Menches. Seems that in 1892, he tapped into the mother load of grease at the Summit County Fair with his own creation. When a pork delivery failed to materialize one busy morning, the Menches brothers were left lacking the main ingredient for their famous sausage sandwiches. Snorting their noses at the adversity, they substituted ground beef. With zeal, circular hunks were flavored, formed, and fired. In the spirit of saving the day in the "last minute" (all too prevalent in food folklore), Frank Menches began slapping patties between the two halves of buns and proceeded to canonize himself as the "inventor" of the hamburger.

Even more colorful is the "just in the nick of time story" handed down to descendants of Louis Lassen, once famed burgermeister of Louis' Lunch in New Haven, Connecticut. According to Ken Lassen, current owner and grandson of the founder, an unidentified man came waltzing in at the turn of the century and requested a "quick" sandwich. Ever ready to please, his grandfather mashed a handful of sliced meat trimmings into a single patty, cooked it in a vertical broiler, and slipped it in between—you guessed it—two slices of bread!

Is there really one birthplace of the hamburger? No one will ever know for certain. In all probability, the hamburger sandwich invented itself—created simultaneously by a melting pot of individuals who happened to tune into the universal consciousness of human inventiveness, imagination, and hunger. ∎

"Hamburger" Charlie Nagreen
Seymour, Wisconsin, resident Charlie Nagreen is one of many claimants to the right of "hamburger inventor." Seems it all started somewhere around 1885, when 15-year-old Charlie began peddling chopped beef to the throng of hungry visitors attending the Outgamie County Fair. Courtesy Tom Duffey, Home of the Hamburger, Inc.

The All-American Hamburger
Served, as usual, with a side of French fries and dill pickle. Martin R. Jones, Unicorn Stock Photos

Takhoma-Burger
Right, "We didn't invent the hamburger, we just perfected it!" Another claim from a mom-and-pop operation in Wichita, Kansas, that still manages to capture the public's interest. "Takhoma-Burger" is a derivative of the Steak n Shake catch-word "Takhomasak," first popularized in the Midwest during the late thirties to describe the chain's convenient, "four-way service."

Louis' Lunch
Louis' Lunch in New Haven, Connecticut, is one of the American establishments that claims to have originated the hamburger. Reportedly, an unidentified man came in and requested a "quick" sandwich at the turn of the century. Burgermeister Louis Lassen formed a lump of meat trimmings into a patty, cooked it on a broiler, and slipped it between bread! The burger was born.

**DAILY NEWS, Los Angeles II
FRIDAY, OCT. 5, 1951**

Hamburger inventor dies

AKRON, O., Oct. 5. - (U.P.) - Concessionaire Frank Menches, who is credited with "inventing" the hamburger, died here today at the age of 86.

Menches ended his active life as concessionaire for county fairs here in 1938, but not until after he had left his mark on the gastronomic habits of the nation.

Before the turn of the century, Menches entered the concession business. At the Summit County (Akron) fair in 1892, Menches nearly ran out of sausage. In an effort to please his customers, he ground up a sausage and sold it as a cooked, meat patty.

It was unexplainably named "hamburger" about two years later.

That concoction, plus his introduction and manufacture of ice cream cones here from the world's fair of 1903, brought Menches a small fortune.

*B*y the early 1900s, the hamburger had gained a rather inauspicious reputation. Like the hot dog, the true composition of cooked burger was difficult to determine by mere sight or bite.

continued from page 48
sight or bite. Claims for purity were rarely made, the description on signs and chalkboards merely reading "hamburg." Gristle, bone, scraps of fat, and even horse meat became the backroom filler for the most disreputable grill men. Public suspicion deterred

sales and focused on the short-order cook with his secret cabinet of "hamburger helpers."

Of course not all of America's burger stands resorted to padding their ground beef; there were many reputable operations in business. Even so, while some excelled by using quality ingredients and sanitary methods, they

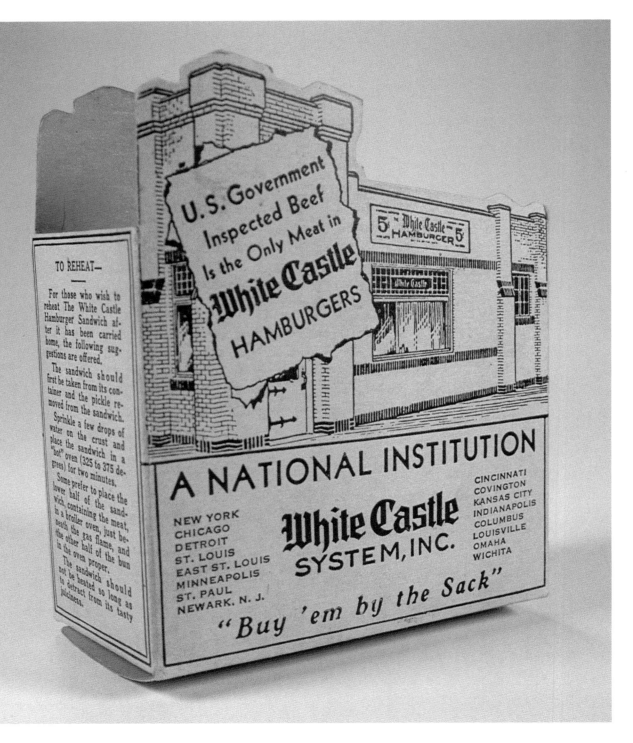

White Castle Hamburger Holder
White Castle hamburgers were small, often cradled in a paper container for easy hand-holding. From the Chuck Sturm Collection

failed in the most basic culinary arts. Self-taught operators often cooked their flattened meatballs too long, resulting in a grilled patty that lacked any flavor or moistness. Unskilled cooking procedures rendered even the finest ground chuck into a tasteless mass of meat. The result was a dried-out patty that required a prodigious amount of ketchup to lubricate its journey through the esophagus.

Fortunately, Anderson was handy with a spatula and griddle. Before his arrival in Kansas, he fine-tuned his short-order shtick in numerous hash houses across the land. Through a combination of hard work and experience, he learned how to get the most out of a lump of ground beef. To the ordinary observer, his method appeared as a simple manipulation of materials: instead of forming thick wads of minced meat and forcing them to fruition upon hot metal, he fashioned his patties thin. With high heat on the griddle, he

Building a White Castle
During their heyday in the thirties, White Castle hamburger buildings were constructed on location. Simple in design, they were completed almost as fast as you could slice a pickle for garnish. Courtesy of Kings-X Inc.

Retired White Castle
Left, by the fifties, the porcelain-covered White Castle stand became a fixture on many American street corners. This stand was retired from hamburger service in Minneapolis in the eighties and replaced by a new, back-lit-panel stand—but the old stand was moved to a new lot and continues to do business as an office. Michael Dregni

Modern White Castle
Today's White Castle stands literally glow in the dark with back-lit panels and flood lighting. This modern stand on East Lake Street in Minneapolis retained the old-fashioned sign of the stand it replaced. Michael Dregni

seared them quickly on both sides, sealing in flavor. At the same time, a small amount of shredded onions was mashed into the sizzle. Two halves of a bun followed, coming to rest over the steaming meat as it finished cooking. As grease dripped over the side of his grill (it didn't have edges to trap the fat), the bread assimilated the aromatic meat and onion vapors, capturing flavors usually lost to the air.

The public responded favorably to Anderson's burger methodology and within months, his flavorful hamburgers became the lunchtime feed for Kansas workers. The remodeled streetcar quickly became too cramped to serve the crowds and a much larger shop was opened in the summer of 1920. Soon, a third Anderson burger outlet followed. Apparently, he was doing something

right; his little nickel-apiece hamburgers were disappearing as fast as he could have the fresh meat and buns delivered.

Finally, Anderson decided that it was time to expand the horizons of his steamed onion burger and make a name for it in the marketplace. He was short on funds, and teamed up with local real estate and insurance man Edgar Waldo "Billy" Ingram to enlarge the operation. With a $700 loan and a lot of optimism, Anderson constructed his fourth, and most memorable, burger emporium in March of 1921.

Following the design of his third stand, the new building was constructed completely from rusticated concrete block. But instead of forming a simple rectangle with concrete stones and leaving it at that, he decided to edge the roofline with a crenelated arrangement. The results were attention-getting: the small building instantly recalled images of a castle. However, the imperial design didn't stop there. At one corner of the roof, a tiny tower was erected of the same material. Reminiscent of the medieval days of knights and chivalry, it provided the diminutive building the visual wallop required to stand out. The exterior was painted a bright white and above the single door and window combination were painted the words "White Castle Hamburgers," with the five-cent price. Coined by Ingram, the majestic title lent a heightened level of respectability to the hamburger, one that conjured up associations of purity, uniformity, and strength.

As White Castle spread to cities throughout the country, "Buy 'em by the Sack" soon became the slogan for the burgerization of America. Although it was a long battle, the tainted image of yesterday's dubious burgers began to fade, replaced by scenes of bright white porcelain, gleaming countertops, polished metal, and freshly scrubbed employees. By 1931, 115 units from Wichita to New York City provided customers friendly service within the same spic and span surroundings. Now, identical juicy onion burgers were served on identical counters and consumed on identical stools, regardless of the location.

The success didn't go unnoticed for long. Imitators copied the format right down to the

continued on page 59

"Buy 'em by the Sack" soon became the slogan for the burgerization of America. It was a long battle but the tainted image of yesterday's dubious burgers faded— replaced by scenes of bright white porcelain, gleaming countertops, polished metal, and freshly scrubbed employees.

Hamburgers and Coca-Cola
Always available at the sign of the White Castle. Michael Dregni

HAMBURGER ARCHITECTURE

Hamburgers made their debut on the food scene as irregular lumps of chopped beef, hand shaped according to the improvisational jazz of lunch counter short order. During the early years, long before the cookie-cutter aesthetics of the Big Mac came into vogue, concerns over circular uniformity and ingredients were minimal.

When fry-by-the-seat-of-your-pants legends Charlie Nagreen and Frank Menches formed ground round for the griddle, personal artistry ensured that every burger was a unique one. Irregularly molded perimeters of meat—with one piece more or less hanging out at one side or the other—didn't affect taste. At the time, it was all part of their appeal.

Redeemed of their dubious reputation by the mid-1930s, the individuality of America's beef patties slowly waned. Suddenly, the proprietors of roadside food businesses followed the preparatory parameters of the White Castle outlets. Mixing in just the right amount of fat became a major concern, the quality of meat of utmost importance. Approved by the public, the unvarying look of the "assembly line" became the credo for hamburger standardization.

Aiding this quest for a perfect burger blob, manufacturers of restaurant equipment soon introduced a useful arsenal of kitchen gadgetry. The Sanitary Hamburger Press Company marketed a hand-operated device capable of producing meat cakes possessing identical specifications. With the speed and accuracy of three hyperactive butchers, eleven precise "patties" of meat could now be extracted from just one pound of grind.

For even the most addle-minded burgermeister, creating an exacting

Sanitary Hamburger Press
As the ad promised, "Makes all hamburger cakes of uniform size."

The Imp Broil-O-Matic
Labor-saving devices like this Broil-O-Matic were just the thing for the small-time operator of roadside refreshment stands. In one, compact unit, hamburgers and hot dogs, etc., could be cooked up without a lot of equipment.

The visual aspects of the hamburger were re-energized when restauranteur Bob Wian created his famous double-decker creation in 1937.
By simply adding a center slice of bun, what had fast become a mundane marriage of beef and bread was elevated to a new level.

The Famous Double-Decked Delight
The famous Big Boy double-deck burger circa 1970 taken at the Sepulveda Boulevard Bob's in San Fernando, a California drive-in now part of street history. After Bob Wian created his Big Boy hamburger in 1937, the craze for double-decker hamburgers galvanized the nation. Soon, there were "Boy" theme burger bars everywhere. Imitators followed, introducing sandwiches named the Beefy Boy, Fat Boy, Chubby Boy, Bun Boy, Country Boy, Husky Boy, Brawny Boy, Lucky Boy, Super Boy, Hi Boy, and a long list of others. ©1994 Kent Bash

succession of identical "hamburger sandwiches" was now second nature. Anybody could do it: a minced batch of meat was loaded into one end and a crank was turned. Extruded wheels of beef, 3 1/2 inches in diameter by 1/4 inch thick plopped out from its bottom—untouched by human hands! The age of burger boredom had officially arrived.

Fortunately, the visual aspects of the hamburger were re-energized when restauranteur Bob Wian created his famous double-decker creation in 1937. By simply adding a center slice of bun, what had fast become a mundane marriage of beef and bread was elevated to a new level. In a perfect example of art imitating life— or in this case food mimicking architecture—multiple stories of beef, lettuce, cheese, relish, and sesame seed bun resulted in what would become the motoring crowd's ultimate Dagwood.

Reincarnated as a fast-food representation of the streamlined designs typical of Simon's, Herbert's, Carpenter's, and a long list of structures being erected to serve customers within their chariots, the once-disreputable hamburger attained an aura all its own. All grown up and dressed to the hilt, it was a "Big Boy" now—a hand-held monument to American ingenuity and culinary pluck.

By the 1950s, hundreds of millions of hamburgers were being sold each year. Coming as no surprise, the popularity of hot dogs, barbecue, grilled cheese, chili con carne, steak sandwiches, and even the chipped beef platter fell quickly to a position at the bottom of the menu. The culture born of the motorcar finally had a food it could hold in one hand and still eat while driving the strip.

Portable, palatable packages perfectly suited for eating-on-the-go, hamburger sandwiches are now solidly established for all forms of bench-seat snacking. To this day, they continue to sizzle as the quintessential staple of the American road. ∎

Hamburger Heaven
Wimpy would have swooned at the sight of this hot, neon hamburger. It smells so good one can almost see it.

continued from page 55

buns and soon there were all kinds of eateries adhering to similar methods of standardization. The proprietors of America's car-oriented eateries were paying close attention; those with foresight borrowed what features they could and nominated the cooked wafer of beef nestled between two fluffs of bread to become the new candidate for "roadfood most likely to succeed."

The Central States, California, and Texas were now well on their way to serving the hungry within their cars. But, the East Coast regions lagged behind in accommodating four-wheeled diners. That was understandable; since a brief warm season limited most outdoor activity to a few short months, it just

made better sense to remain with the established norm of indoor eating. More important,

continued on page 64

Kings-X Canvas and Ribbed Tower
In 1938, the White Castle hamburger chain decided to close down all of its restaurants west of the Mississippi. Andrew James King was employed by the square burger maker at the time, ten years under his belt as head of research and development. As principle "idea-man" for the company, it was his responsibility to develop new products and devise advertising promotions. When Billy Ingram announced he was moving the Castle's headquarters to Columbus, Ohio, King declined. He bought out the three Wichita White Castle locations and decided to try his own luck in the burger business. Later he expanded his holdings to other locations, opening Kings-X Drive-Ins and coffee-shop restaurants. Jimmie King's son Wayne used to work as a Kings-X carhop when he was a kid and often reminisces about the good times. Fridays are particularly memorable: Catholics couldn't eat the burgers, so cars began to pile into the lot by 9pm and proceeded to order a glass of water or a Coke. Straight up at midnight, car headlamps began to flash and horns would honk. Suddenly, everyone wanted a hamburger! For the Kings-X curb server, Fridays were rough. This unit built during the late fifties is still standing at Kellogg and Oliver in Wichita. Today, it is known as Livingston's. Courtesy of Kings-X Inc.

Kings-X Chicken Meal Box
Left, during the fifties, Kings-X manager Jack Bowman came up with an idea for a "chicken special." Wichita customers loved the special so much that they couldn't keep up with the demand. People were waiting in line until they closed, all there for the chicken meal. Courtesy Kings-X Inc., Hal Pottorf photographer

BOB'S BIG BOY BURGER

*"Wian plopped on some relish, and began stacking up
a ridiculous caricature of the hamburger—a double-decked delight
pushing burger creativity to the outer limits!"*

Robert Wian learned the restaurant business the hard way. When his father's furniture business in California faltered during the early thirties, he took a job washing dishes at the White Log Tavern to help out. Although fresh from high school, it didn't take long for him to become manager. His experience was soon rolled over into a better job at the Rite Spot, a Glendale

Bob Wian Behind Counter
Robert C. Wian was the brains and brawn behind the counter of a ten-stool hamburger stand he purchased from two little old ladies in 1936. To raise the money he needed to buy this Glendale, California, eatery, he sold his prized possession, a 1933 DeSoto. Unfortunately, the sale only netted him $300—the women were asking $350! He scraped up the balance, consummated the deal, and ventured forth into hamburger history. The burger bar was promptly renamed "Bob's Pantry." Courtesy Richard McLay

eatery favored by Angelinos. There, he learned all the rules of the eating-out game—realizing along the way that he had a growing desire to become his own boss.

When two elderly ladies considered selling out their ten-stool lunch counter on Colorado Boulevard, Wian saw his opportunity. Still, he had to make a painful decision: sell his prized 1933 DeSoto roadster to get the bulk of the $350 asking price or pass over the deal. It was a clear choice. The car found a new owner and Wian got the money he needed. The eatery was his! He renamed it Bob's Pantry and began to work the counter alone.

Members of Chuck Foster's Orchestra adopted the Pantry as a late-night hangout and stopped in after gigs. High school pals of Wian's felt comfortable there, filling up with numerous hamburgers, gallons of Hires root beer, and packets of cigarettes. One frosty night in February of 1937, bass musician Stewie Strange became bored with the usual midnight snack and uttered the historic question, now ensconced in legend: "How about something different for a change, Bob?"

In a teasing mood, Wian was quick to accommodate. He proceeded to cut a sesame seed bun into three slices and flipped two burgers onto the griddle. While the meat sizzled, the band watched in fascination as leaves of lettuce and slices of cheese were readied on the sideboard. Finally, the cooked patties were lifted from the hot plate. Wian plopped on some relish, and began stacking up a ridiculous caricature of the hamburger—a double-decked delight pushing burger creativity to the outer limits. The band loved it!

A few days later, chunky Richard Woodruff wandered in through the front door. He lived down the street and often came in to sweep the floor and perform other busy work for Wian. Only six years old, he was already exhibiting a "Wimpy"-sized appetite for hamburgers—with a stomach to match. He figured out his own way to get them and charmed both the lunchtime customers and Wian with his plump physique and droopy overalls. It came as no surprise to the regulars why Bob Wian christened his unique sandwich the "Big Boy!"

After a local cartoonist sketched a rendition of the urchin on a napkin, the tousled hair and chubby cheeks became a trademark adorning the front facade. News of the great-tasting "double-deck" cheeseburger spread and within three years, Wian opened a second eatery in Los Angeles. By 1949, he was franchising his sandwich (and its youthful mascot) to operators in a half-dozen states. Meanwhile, a trio of his own Big Boy dinettes prospered. Featuring "snappy service" drive-in lanes and inside seating, their transitional design bridged the carhop era with the coming age of coffee-shops. In 1964, Wian's built his last open-air unit.

A few years later, McDonald's franchisee Jim Delligatti wanted to bring out a "new" idea for a sandwich when he remembered Wian's tasty double.

Bob's Pantry Exterior
When local bass player Stewie Strange asked for something different one night in 1937, Bob Wian created a new burger sensation at the spur of the moment. The double-deck cheeseburger was an immediate sensation and was later dubbed the "Big Boy," inspired by local lad and burger biter Richard Woodruff. A local cartoonist sketched the portly kid on a napkin and forever immortalized the image of Wian's stacked delight. Courtesy Richard McLay

Bob's Big Boy Carhops and Interior
Right, the carhops at Bob Wian's first drive-in wore a number of different uniforms before settling on one style. The western-style outfit with hat was one of the earliest variations. The setup men behind the counter, or "Boyfriends" as they were later referred to, stuck with the established norm of black tie and disposable paper wedge-cap. Courtesy of June Wian

Toluca Lake Bob's Neon Sign
The Bob's Big Boy restaurant in Toluca Lake, California, has managed to elude the wrecking ball. When a building in Los Angeles survives for more than forty years, it's a remarkable accomplishment. During the early 1990s, the state designated the 43-year-old restaurant as an official "California Point of Historical Interest." ©1994 Kent Bash

Bob's Big Boy Menu
Right, updated version of the early cut-out menu, circa early 1940s. The Big Boy was slowly becoming more refined.
Courtesy Richard McLay

HOME OF THE
BIG BOY HAMBURGERS

Bob's

Famous for
HAMBURGERS
CHILI • STEAKS
THICK MALTS
THIN PANCAKES

2 Locations

900 E. COLORADO
GLENDALE

624 S. SAN FERNANDO RD.
BURBANK

The Big Boy Combo

At highway dining facilities such as those on the Garden State Turnpike in New Jersey, the Big Boy can still be found. There, plastic banks are sold as souvenirs. Elias Brothers is a chain of Big Boy hamburger franchisees operating in Michigan. From the Chuck Sturm collection

During the fifties, he managed a West Coast drive-in and was impressed by the numerous imitators of the twin burger. Whether influenced by nostalgia or imagination remains unclear. What's certain is that he developed a close copy of the bi-level Big Boy. Later, he admitted that the conception of this burger clone "wasn't like discovering the light bulb—the bulb was already there...all I did was screw it in the socket."

This Big "Mac" was introduced nationwide at McDonald s outlets in 1968. It was an immediate hit, soon accounting for 19 percent of sales! But, that was no surprise for Robert C. Wian, Jr. His double-decked sandwich—created at the spur of the moment to satisfy the desire for something different—had already built a food empire. Another variation on the theme couldn't hurt. He—and everyone else acquainted with hamburger history—would always know the Big Boy was Bob's. ∎

Bob's Big Boy Drive-In

Robert Wian opened this California drive-in around 1947. Bob's Home of the Big Boy really hit the big time, complete with interior coffee-shop and separate curb-service facilities. Courtesy of June Wian

continued from page 59

the diverse range of popular foods available in the Atlantic States proved a difficult menu to breach with plain ol' burgers and barbecue. Fried clams, pizza pies, gyros, and an assortment of other delights often relegated beef—whether fried, boiled, steamed, or baked—to last choice.

All of that was about to change.

In the summer of 1927, J. Willard Marriott was on his way from Utah to Washington, D.C. on a quest to make his own fortune in the food business. A young Mormon elder with a cowboy background and college education, he figured the nation's capitol was an ideal place to start—since it was "big and hot" and receptive to root beer. Fortunately, a friend

The Chuc Wagun
The Chuc Wagun was an early predecessor to the Arby's chain. Wheel-Burgers and Hub-Burgers could be had for a mere 15¢ during the forties. Was axle grease used as a topping? Courtesy of Kings-X Inc.

from Utah who was currently studying law in the Capitol City agreed. He matched Marriott's three-grand investment and a root beer stand partnership was formed.

By this time, the name A&W had already gained a measure of brand recognition. The aggressive franchising of its flavorful concentrate to independent operators created a quick expansion in Northern California, Utah, and Texas. Hundreds of operators had already built substantial businesses on the nickel mug of root beer; by 1933, there were 171 A&Ws doing business nationwide. Marriott and his partner were well aware of the success, as A&W refreshment stands were among the first

to appear in their home state. Although A&W was not yet established in the competitive East Coast markets, they surmised it would be a worthwhile investment.

The optimistic pair became the first to obtain the rights to sell A&W in the Washington area and opened a hole-in-the-wall operation on Fourteenth Street NW and Park Road. As anticipated, business proved to be excellent during the tepid months of summer. However, when autumn breezes turned to brisk winds, the appeal of ice cold soft drinks plummeted. Concerned about her husband's livelihood, Marriott's wife Alice suggested that the men

continued on page 72

Chicken in the Rough
Chicken in the Rough was invented in 1936 by Mr. and Mrs. Beverly Osborne. They ran a small Oklahoma City drive-in and franchised their tasty poultry dish to operators throughout the nation. Consisting of one-half of a golden brown chicken served with shoestring potatoes, hot buttered biscuits, and a jug o' honey, it was a meal served without silverware. In 1958, Chicken in the Rough could be purchased for $1.40 Tuesday through Sunday, reduced to $1.00 on the Monday "family night." Courtesy Chuck Sturm

STORY OF THE COCA-COLA CLASSIC

On the Spring afternoon of May 8, 1886, inventor Dr. John Styth Pemberton toiled over a three-legged brass cauldron in the backyard of his ante-bellum house on Atlanta's Marietta Street. Gingerly stirring a thick, syrupy mixture of sugar and flavorings over an open fire, he was on the verge of a breakthrough that would one day awaken the taste-buds of an entire nation and receive accolades from around the globe.

The experimental brew was originally intended to improve "French Wine of Coca," a bitter nostrum for headaches that Pemberton previously developed for drugstores. To his surprise, the reformulated ingredients exceeded the best taste expectations he could imagine. With great enthusiasm, he hastened to share the delicious news with his other business partners.

Upon tasting the creation and inquiring of its ingredients, Pemberton's partner, bookkeeper Frank Robinson, sat down and penned today's ubiquitous "Coca-Cola" trademark in flowing Spencerian script. Armed with a catchy new name, a striking trademark, and a gallon jug topped off with the sweet mixture, Pemberton headed east towards Jacobs' Pharmacy to begin marketing his product.

Hoisting the jug upon the counter, he offered proprietor Venable and landlord Jacobs a sample of his new concoction. Three glasses were taken down from the back bar and filled with the syrup, then chilled water, in careful proportions of one to five. As tumblers emptied, three faces beamed with unanimous satisfaction as all proceeded to sing praises for this wonderful new delight!

As the legend goes, a second round of drinks was called for, with Venable absent-mindedly shooting carbonated water into the glasses. But whether by accident or design, the fizzy combination unquestionably produced a far superior drink. According to Pemberton, it was just the catalyst required to pull the full flavor from his sublime kola nut blend.

Despite the success, Pemberton's failing health continued to worsen, forcing him to sell out two-thirds of his rights to Willis Venable and George S. Lowndes. Forthwith, all equipment and ingredients required to manufacture the syrup were trucked from his home to the pharmacy's basement. Eventually, local businessman Asa Candler sampled the formula and bought up all the rights to the process for a mere $2,300. In 1892, he incorporated the Coca-Cola Company.

The new entity instituted an aggressive plan for marketing, canvassing the South with colorful fountain signs and free sample tickets. By 1899, decorative advertising clocks, porcelain fountain urns, posters, calendars, and even serving trays became visible marketing tools. Bell-shaped glasses imprinted with the Coca-Cola logo were added to the list of premiums and within a few years, salesmen had soda fountains and restaurants

Jacobs' Pharmacy circa 1900s
Jacobs' Pharmacy as it appeared during the soda fountain's prime when the first glass of Coca-Cola was sold in 1886. The ornate fountain area was usually situated in the center of the drugstore, capturing the attention of all who entered. Courtesy of The Coca-Cola Company

Pretty Girl Tray
From 1894 to 1904, the Massengale Advertising Agency of Atlanta handled advertising for Coca-Cola. While the lithographic posters, calendars, and intricately detailed serving trays of the era were considered works of art, they appeared somewhat dated by the "modern" 1900s. In 1904, the D'Arcy agency took over Coca-Cola advertising and revamped the "pretty girl" image. Still elegantly dressed in her long frocks, she began appearing in more casual surroundings including scenes at the beach, playing tennis, riding in a horse and buggy, and floating in a rowboat. This 1897 "Victorian Girl" Coca-Cola serving tray is the oldest example known to exist.
Courtesy of The Coca-Cola Company

displaying all variations of the mark.

With the popularization of the "Ritz Boy" billboard in 1925 and a variety of catchy ad campaigns, Coca-Cola became a highly recognized brand at virtually every drugstore, gas station, and luncheonette. When the distinctive fluted bottle became a registered trademark in 1960, the bubbly formulation it held was already an established favorite of customers patronizing drive-ins and the raft of walk-ups spreading nationwide.

For the modern-day motorist, Coca-Cola's curvaceous container became permanently linked with the pleasure of grabbing a burger and a bag of fries. Along most of America's main streets, country roads, and two-lane highways, the familiar cursive lettering gracing green-tinted decanters now stood for just one thing: Coke...the pause that refreshes! ∎

Coke Bottle Development

When soft drink bottling was in its infancy, beer bottles and cork stoppers were the only materials available. As demand for specialty bottles grew, W. H. Hutchinson & Son of Chicago dominated the field. Initially, internal ball stoppers replaced cork. To break the seal, one pushed on the ball and with a "pop" it would drop to the bottom of the bottle. Hutchinson improved on this version with a patented spring stopper, featuring a wire-loop permanently attached to a flat metal disk. A gentle push downward released the bottle's contents. The automatic resealing feature preserved the fizz of any leftovers. From left to right: (1) 1894, the first acknowledged Coca-Cola bottler was a

Vicksburg, Mississippi, man named Joseph A. Biedenharn. "Blob-top" Hutchinson bottles embossed with "Coca-Cola" are extremely rare, since it was not customary to imprint contents on early soda bottles. (2) 1899–1902, another Hutchinson-style bottle used briefly by early bottlers (note the wire-loop stopper). (6) 1915, the first glass package using the classic contour design Bottle patented in 1915 and introduced to the public in 1916. This classic contour design is still in use today. (10) 1975, experimental plastic bottle, never marketed. (11) 1961 to present, the no-return glass bottle. Courtesy of The Coca-Cola Company

Baird Coca-Cola Premium Clock
This clock, offered as a premium, reflects the ambivalence of early advertising associated with Coca-Cola. On the one hand it proclaims a "refreshing beverage" while on the other extolling its virtues as a "headache and nerve tonic"; this ambiguity was probably due to the syrup's early association with the pharmaceutical business. Around 1904, Coca-Cola's advertising finally broke free from the "medicinal" claims and concentrated exclusively on refreshment. This Chicago-era Baird Clock premium with eight day movement was manufactured between 1896–1900. Courtesy of The Coca-Cola Company

*O*n May 8, 1886, inventor Dr. John Styth Pemberton toiled over a three-legged brass cauldron in the backyard of his ante-bellum house in Atlanta. This experimental brew was originally intended to improve "French Wine of Coca," a bitter nostrum for headaches that Styth previously developed for drugstores.

BE REALLY REFRESHED...DRIVE-IN FOR COKE!

Brighten every bite with Coke! Only Coca-Cola gives you that cheerful lift...that cold crisp taste! No wonder it's the real refreshment...anytime...anywhere you're driving! Pause...for Coke!

SIGN OF GOOD TASTE

"COKE" IS A REGISTERED TRADE-MARK. COPYRIGHT © 1959 THE COCA-COLA COMPANY.

Seventeen—August, 1959

231

Two Kids With Coke and Food Tray
Clean-cut all-American kids at the drive-in, circa 1969. Courtesy of The Coca-Cola Company

LORRAINE MAGOWAN, SIMON'S DRIVE-IN

In 1938, Lorraine Magowan went down to Wiggin's Trade School in Los Angeles to enroll. That day, a man hiring for Simon's Drive-In was out at the school recruiting workers. Already experienced as a waitress, Lorraine hooked an interview that later culminated in a job. She would become part of the Simon's Drive-In team at the new Wilshire and Santa Monica location. While Lorraine always dreamed of waitressing at the Brown Derby (a movie-star haven), she soon discovered a job at Simon's was the next best thing.

Back then, Simon's posted two carhops at each side of the parking lot and instructed the girls to call out "CI" ("car in") whenever a customer pulled up on their side. Lorraine spied a black sportscar approaching and made the call to claim her first outside customer. To her delight, screen star George Raft was in the driver's seat—Betty Grable his passenger! She remembers thinking, "I hope they don't want an inside tray" and fortunately, the pair opted for a chocolate malt. It was served unspilled by an excited Lorraine.

Another night, an elderly couple wheeled in and decided that they wanted to dine in the backseat of their car. Trays of food were delivered and the couple began eating when suddenly the sedan began rolling backwards! Before they could swallow a bite, Lorraine hopped into the front seat and slammed on the brakes! For a carhop, it was a heroic effort, garnering her a 50¢ tip for her efforts (that was a big one in those days). Today, Lorraine channels that early energy by volunteering at the local hospital and remaining active through her mid-seventies. Her early days at Simon's Drive-In have proven invaluable; she's indisputable proof that former carhops only get better with age. ∎

Paul's Bowls
Located at California and K in Bakersfield, California, Paul's Drive-In (run by Clif and Eddie) provided many souvenirs. Because of the acquisitive nature of the car diner, a few good examples exist today. From the Chuck Sturm Collection

Early Hot Shoppe
Lower right, while the tamales sold at J. Willard Marriott's original "hole-in-the-wall" stand on Fourteenth Street NW and Park Road in Washington, D. C. were eventually replaced with more popular entrees, the name somehow stuck. Later, when his chain of drive-ins was in full swing, running boys and waitresses cried out the imaginary order "Big Tamale!" whenever Mr. Marriott appeared. For the staff, it was a humorous way of acknowledging and honoring his presence—at the same time alerting others to look sharp. Courtesy Marriott International, Inc.

continued from page 65

add a small selection of sandwiches to their menu, along with some homemade chili and hot tamales. A small hot plate was put in the front window so pedestrians could see and smell the array of goodies.

Passersby were intrigued with the heavenly aroma and showed little resistance to stopping in for a bite. One day, an inquisitive customer asked when the Marriotts were going to open their "hot shop." Unknowingly, he presented the partners with a new name for their enterprise. The A&W logo on the front facade was soon joined by the words "The Hot Shoppe," painted in cursive lettering on the front window and overhead awning.

Marriott manned the counter area while his wife cooked tamales and ran the register. The combination of warm foods and cold root beer clicked: in the first year, their modest operation took in an admirable $16,000. The

business prospered and in less than two years, Marriott opened the first drive-in restaurant in the East. "Food For The Whole Family" served in your car caught on fast and by 1930 Marriott had three drive-in Hot Shoppes operating at full tilt. Visitors in automobiles loved the huge parking lots, the friendly "running boys," and the classy dessert called the hot fudge ice cream cake. Before long, Marriott's combination of orange roof tiles and familiar A&W logo became synonymous with East Coast car service.

Meanwhile, the hamburger, hot dog, and barbecue kings operating in California were making plans to inject new life into their own car-stands. Los Angeles was a city made by the automobile, with plenty of restauranteurs eager to capitalize on the year-round sunshine and general acceptance of new ideas. As development changed the face of the roadside in the car's own image, the simple structures erected almost a decade ago were becoming increasingly boring. The wide, endless boulevards and extensive network of surface streets now sprawling in every direction demanded something better: a new style, a new look—one to match the glamour of this starstruck city.

When Mr. Harry Carpenter, a brilliant operator from Texas, arrived in Los Angeles during the Depression years, he was impressed by the expansive boulevards and took note of the vacant lots available at busy corners. There were already a number of Pig Stands doing business in the area, albeit with modest structures of octagonal design a bit larger than a couple of Model As parked bumper to bumper. Despite their modest architecture, they were doing an admirable business—

Hot Shoppe and Polar Bear
When the sale of alcohol was repealed in 1933, the Hot Shoppes became outlets for liquor. At one particular unit, the police got a call about a riot when a man insisted on dropping empty glasses to the pavement. The curb manager pulled him from the car and knocked him sprawling—soon to be joined by fifty curb boys and customers, all swinging. Later, when a carhop was handed money for some limeades used by a car full of men as chasers, one tipsy passenger asked, "Does that take care of everything?" "Yes, everything but something for the boy," replied the carhop. "We gotta take care of the boy!" said one of the men. He climbed out of the car and proceeded to smash a whisky bottle over the carhop's head! Courtesy Library of Congress

something Carpenter was quick to point out to his brother Charles. The observation was duly noted and the pair continued scouting locations for a series of eateries that would extrapolate the curb service idea further than ever before.

The Carpenters' most memorable sandwich stand opened at the cross-streets of Sunset and Vine in the early thirties, causing quite a stir for locals accustomed to the spartan accoutrements of the current haunts. As later reported in a 1946 issue of *The Diner*, Carpenter "dressed up this basic idea [of in-car dining] with typical Hollywood glitter. He paved his lot, put up a building that looked like a cross between the Taj Mahal and Mary Pickford's swimming pool bath-house and found a batch of would-be stars starving to death while waiting for the big chance." Carpenter's became the car-dining derivation of the Yucca-Vine Market, a well-known Los Angeles landmark designed in 1928 by architect Lloyd Wright, son of Frank Lloyd Wright.

Glorifying the subdued design of the Pig Stands, the Carpenter brothers took the format of drive-in dining into the fast lane. The carhops even had their own training films! Featuring an octagonal floorplan with stepped layers, the car-accommodating kiosk became a feeding trough for harried motorists hankering for a quick fifteen-cent hamburger. Not one inch was spared for advertising: a profusion of signs inset into the stepped layers broadcast the availability of "sit 'n eat" sandwiches, chili con carne, barbecued beef, fruit pies, and an assortment of beverages.

At the same time, Bill Simon was running a small chain of dairy lunch counters in Los Angeles. Bill happened to be poker buddies with Harry Carpenter and "Rusty" McDonnell (another local restauranteur, no relation to the McDonald brothers). As the story goes, the group had gathered for one of their late-night games when talk turned to the restaurant business and high overhead costs. Simon, who

As development changed the face of the roadside in the car's own image, the simple structures erected almost a decade ago were becoming increasingly boring. The wide, endless boulevards and extensive network of surface streets now sprawling in every direction demanded something better: a new style, a new look.

Octangular Carpenter's
During the early part of the thirties, Harry Carpenter constructed a more decorative version of the Pig Stand at the corner of Sunset and Vine in Los Angeles. With an octagonal layout and stepped design, it was the foreshadowing of more streamlined forms to come. Eventually, the sharp corners would be dropped in favor of the circular motif, a completely round design that was accessible from all angles and offered little visual resistance. Henry E. Huntington Library and Art Gallery

Carpenter's at Night
Harry Carpenter followed the lead of the other operators by the end of the thirties and constructed small circular units of his own. Los Angeles Dairy Lunch counter owner Bill Simon started the trend when he boasted he could build a small unit for under $6500. "Rusty" McDonnell wagered he couldn't do it—but with the help of architect Wayne McAllister, Simon came in under that goal. The rush for small, efficient units was on! Courtesy Library of Congress

Sunset Boulevard Pig Stand
Opposite page, the Pig Stands were one of the first drive-in restaurants to show the Californians just how Texans cooked up delicious barbecue. At night, crowds of cars packed this Sunset and Vine stand to maximum capacity during the thirties. When Harry Carpenter and his brother arrived (also from Texas), they added a little bit of style to the formula. Carpenter's octagonal stand (and neon sign) can be seen in the background. From the collections of the Texas/Dallas History and Archives Division, Dallas Public Library

Lower right,
Circular Drive-In Roof Plan

Roberts at Night
Opposite page, to circumvent local sign ordinances and rules against erecting large illuminated signs on the tops of buildings, many drive-ins incorporated rooftop towers, or pylons as part of their integral structure. Whether adorned with neon lettering, flashing lights, atomic balls, or twisted spirals of light, they attracted the attention of the motorist more readily than any billboard could ever have hoped. "The Burbank" Roberts Brothers drive-in located on Victory and Olive Boulevards featured a twisted flash of what appeared to be electricity at the top of its pylon. With circular design, modern equipment, and air conditioning for inside diners, it was a mecca for motorists in the San Fernando Valley. Courtesy Burbank Historical Society

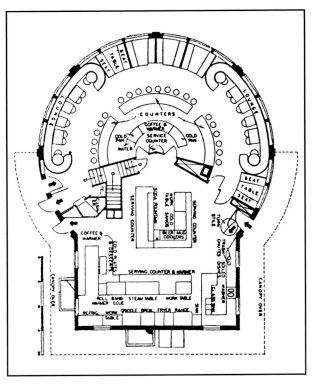

had a few ideas of his own, began bragging that he could open a carhop eatery for only $6,500. His gambling buddies saw a sure bet and wagered it couldn't be done!

Simon accepted the challenge and contracted local architect Wayne McAllister to develop a simple, economical, and eye-catching design. By planning the eatery with small "taxpayer" lots in mind (under 150 feet square), he developed a compact, concentrated version of existing service structures. To utilize every inch of available space, the building followed a circular layout, allowing full utilization without the inefficiencies of a rectangle. The kitchen and rotary barbecue oven were located directly within the center, allowing the carhops and customers to be served from multiple angles. Only twelve stools were provided for the sit-down customers. Even with a "layer cake" roof stepping up to a centrally

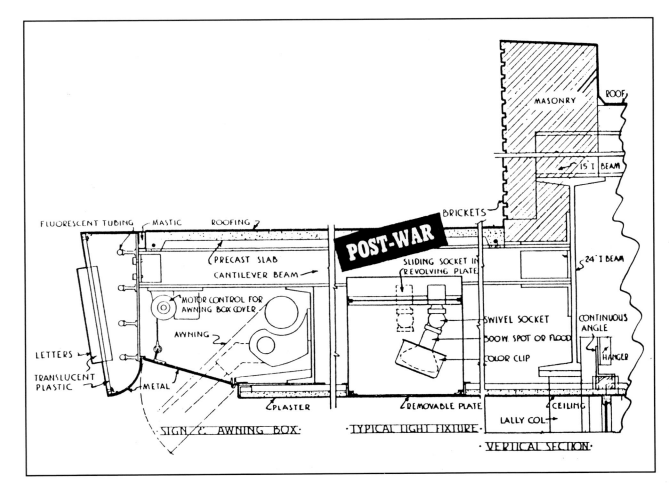

mounted tower, the total cost for the plan came in a little under the goal—an unbelievable victory for Simon! Of course, McAllister helped win Simon's bet—and the confidence of the entire California curb-stand clique.

One by one, the major players switched over to a more softened style, the angular ziggurats of the Art Deco era yielding to purely circular motifs. McAllister's practice thrived and he was soon inundated with work, drawing up similar floor plans for the proprietors of Herbert's, McDonnell's, Roberts', Bob's Big Boy, and even Van de Kamp's. Suddenly, every major intersection in the city of Los Angeles was accented by a circular landmark!

continued on page 86

LIGHTING WITH LUMINOUS NEON

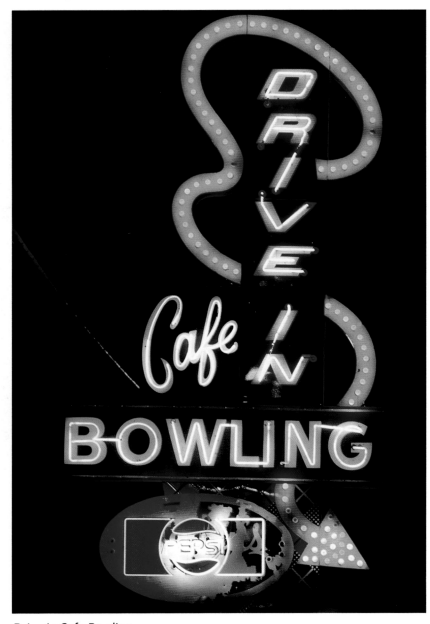

Drive-In Cafe Bowling
Neon hung above a drive-in bowling alley and snack bar in Wichita, Kansas.

Heinrich Geissler devised one of the first genuine prototypes of the non-filament lamp in 1856. Employing high voltage alternating current, he excited carbon dioxide gas trapped within a glass tube to create light. Unknowingly, a magic genie was released from a bottle, one that would eventually become part of the art and architecture of the American road.

Although Geissler's first lamp was an efficient source of illumination, it had one major drawback: The energized gas had a tendency to react chemically with the power electrodes, causing their eventual deterioration. Pressure dropped and the depleted tubes began to sputter.

Fortunately, former Edison employee D. McFarland Moore solved the pressure problem. A device designed to replenish gas lost as electrodes broke down became part of his improved light tubes. Confident of their extended lifespan, he sold his first commercial sign installation to a Newark, New Jersey, hardware store in 1904. Filled with atmospheric gas, it became the precursor of the "neon" sign.

Georges Claude continued experimenting with Moore's tubes in France. Rare distillations like neon and argon gas were substituted for carbon dioxide. When electrically excited with high voltage, neon was found to glow fiery red, argon a grayish blue. Eventually, he introduced a corrosion resistant electrode, registering the revolutionary design patent in 1915. Now, neon-filled tubing could hold its pressure indefinitely, paving the way for practical applications.

Eight years later, neon officially arrived in the United States. West Coast car dealer Earle Anthony became enlightened to the fragile creations produced by the Claude Neon Factory in Paris and decided to exploit the colorful signage at his Los Angeles auto dealership. Installed high where passing cars could see, two blue-bordered beauties spelled out the word "Packard" in searing orange script. Enraptured by the ethereal glow of the illuminated tubing, passing vehicles jammed the boulevard.

By 1932, the key patent to the non-corroding electrode expired, clearing the way for neon's proliferation. Free from restrictions, sign shops multiplied—and soon roadside commerce adopted the attention-getting hues of the new light form. By the end of the thirties, the majority of gasoline stations, drugstores, and hamburger drive-ins were bedecked in a kaleidoscope of electrified color.

As its popularity grew, neon lighting was often incorporated into the design scheme of streetside architecture itself. The rounded corners of the Streamline Moderne soon played host to racy rows of glowing glass. Mimicking the speed and movement of passing cars, colored tubes of plasma swooped, swirled, and danced, reinforcing the architectural illusion of forward momentum.

With their car-accommodating designs, drive-in eateries became roadside beacons for dine-in-your-car service. From their structural epicenter, dramatic pylons ribbed in neon bands poked skyward. Vertically arranged lettering cut a message into the night, proclaiming the availability of "Hamburgers" to a procession of vehicles on the strip.

At streetside, advertising signs attained a new boldness. Hand-painted boards became substantial constructions of porcelain-enameled metal and hollow glass pipe. As animated carhops toted idealized renditions of the perfect hamburger, swirling arrows pointed the way to food and fun. America's drive-ins flickered to life, a bold palette of visual excitement lighting the way with a hot, neon buzz. ∎

Sill's Drive-In With Neon
To the casual observer, there could be no disputing the location of Sill's spectacular drive-in: Las Vegas, Nevada. Like some of its gaming counterparts on the Strip, it was packed with as much neon tubing as it could hold and had its own towering carhop at the roadside. When the sun went down, many motorists decided they better not gamble with their appetites—it was Sill's Drive-In for the best food in town. Courtesy Brian Butko

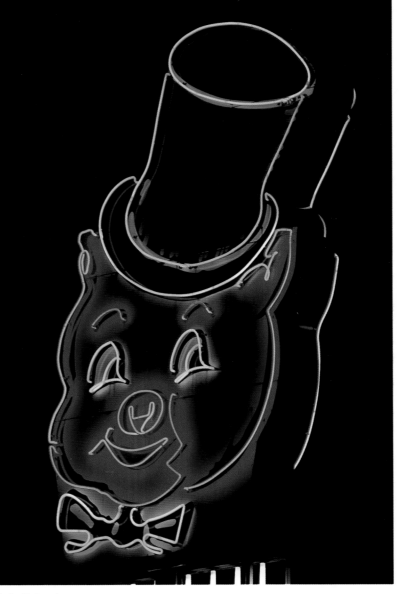

Porky's Drive-In
The pert Porky's pig is a sculpture in neon lighting the night above the famous drive-in in St. Paul, Minnesota. Michael Dregni

Van de Kamp's at Night
Left, the shimmering Van de Kamp's flagship building constructed on Fletcher and San Fernando in Glendale was architect Wayne McAllister's masterpiece. A massive, neon-trimmed delight, it was as much a nighttime confection for the eyes as the ice cream cone was for the lips. Miles of neon tubing outlined virtually every corner and crevice, including the vanes of the life-sized windmill that became the chain's trademark. Because the coffee-shop and bakery were such a success, a pure drive-in was later added on the same lot. With double-kitchens and service outlets, it could accommodate two separate flows of traffic. Later, this same design became the model for Robert Wian's first Big Boy drive-in. Security Pacific National Bank Photograph Collection/Los Angeles Public Library

continued from page 79

From the viewpoint out on the roadway, it appeared that these sculpted structures of chromium, glass, and stainless steel were carefully balanced illusions. Virtually all appeared to defy the laws of gravity with their free-floating overhangs. Many of the front entry areas were actually constructed without doors (Simon's was open twenty-four hours and never closed). Visually, the unified look offered by the circular arrangement transformed what was once a mundane box into a space station for cars. Now, the drive-in dining stand was a circular mecca of neon—conceived, constructed, and operated exclusively for the motorist.

Still, there was more substance to the circular design than just aesthetics. Ever since the days of the original curbside stand, problems with traffic flow and the logistics of serv-

Melody Lanes
The Starlite Room of the Melody Lane drive-in (once a landmark structure located at Wilshire and Western in Los Angeles) served cocktails to (inside) car-customers after the nationwide repeal of Prohibition. For those in need of a Coca-Cola or ham sandwich, an adjoining drive-in provided all the amenities for in-car dining. Security Pacific National Bank Photograph Collection/Los Angeles Public Library

Herbert's Circular by Day
Right, many drive-in restaurants located on the busy cross streets of Los Angeles were considered "taxpayers." Never intended to become permanent landmarks, they typically operated for a short lifespan of ten years or less. As real estate values of these prominent plots rose, the buildings that occupied the space could no longer support the value of the land. Well-known Los Angeles restauranteur Sydney Hoedemaker opened Herbert's Drive-In during the early thirties. Circa 1940, located at Beverly and Fairfax, Los Angeles. Seaver Center for Western History Research, Natural History Museum of Los Angeles County

ing numerous cars were a concern. A completely round design was perfectly suited for the roadside: drivers could easily pull into the parking lot, cruise around the building's periphery, and find a parking space that suited their fancy. Like petals on a flower, automobiles could park around the structure along its entire circumference. Because every space was an equal distance from the kitchen and the curb servers, all were desirable spots (in theory). The "inner circle" eventually assumed a higher status, even though one might have to signal the cars parked behind to leave.

As the restaurants specializing in car food achieved a visual and functional unity by the close of the thirties, the imagery of America's tray toters was also being restyled. As men went off to fight in the war, the pool of

FRONTIER DRIVE IN — 24 HOUR SERVICE
MISSOULA, MONTANA

Frontier Drive In
The Frontier in Missoula, Montana, featured a circular facade combined with a rectangular building and kitchen area circa 1940s. Courtesy Chuck Sturm

Stan's Serve Area with Neon Ceiling
Left, bright neon lighting pulled the customer's eyes right into the front service area of Stan's Fresno drive-in. Beneath the lights, everything was positioned for easy access, including trays, cigarette machines, napkins, and dining utensils. Cooks, or "wheelmen" as they were often referred to, handed food orders directly through small portals to the carhops. At each side, a door allowed customers to enter two separate dining areas. Courtesy Martin Cable, Edwin Schober photographer

Sill's Drive-in Restaurant

5th St. at Charleston Blvd., Las Vegas, Nevada

"Good Food Need Not Be Expensive"

Sill's Drive-In
The Russian launch of the Sputnik on October 4, 1957, triggered more than simply a race for space. Suddenly, American drive-ins mounted satellites, atomic balls, and other futuristic forms atop their rooftop towers. The images of the future held much promise, ideal for the sales of fast-paced foodstuffs such as hamburgers, French fries, and shakes. Sill's Drive-In was ahead of its time with this Las Vegas location, circa late 1940s. Courtesy Chuck Sturm

Gorro Drive Inn
Right, along with the El Sombrero Motel, this border town Tijuana drive-in was perhaps the only circular drive-in ever fashioned in the shape of a sombrero. Circa late 1940s. Courtesy Chuck Sturm

The Gorro Drive Inn and El Sombrero Motel

available workers shifted from male to female. Male carhops became the minority as women took their place at almost every curb-stand, refreshment shack, lunch counter, and burger bar that needed help.

Managers discovered that more hamburgers were sold when served by a pretty face, and before long, the bow-ties and black slacks that typified America's first carhops were replaced by women's service uniforms. At the finest car feeders, carefully assembled outfits became the rage, taking the attire worn by usherettes at the local cinema or hotel bellboy as the standard model. A short waist jacket

became de rigeur, along with coordinating trousers adorned with wide military stripes. At one point, Stanley Burke's California hops donned contrasting uniforms of purple and green, the "Stan's" moniker embroidered right on the shoulder. If portraying a unified image worked well for the petroleum companies, it couldn't hurt the food industry.

The wave of style crested in 1940 when the cover of *Life* magazine featured a full-length cover photograph of Sivils' Drive-Inn girl Josephine Powell, in full-service dress. Taking the showmanship begun at Harry Carpen

continued on page 96

Mark's In & Out Beefburgers
Established in 1954, Mark's has provided a steady supply of 'burgers to hungry drive-in customers in Livingston, Montana—and was still going strong into the 1990s. The large neon sign above the front face of the building promised Montana cattle ranchers that there was no ham in their "beefburgers."
Michael Dregni

THE FABLE OF THE GOLDEN ARCHES

Richard and Maurice McDonald were planning to franchise their successful burger system in 1952. To stand above the visual noise created by miles of drive-ins, motels, car washes, bowling alleys, service stations, and coffee-shops, they decided a new structural style was needed. Without a unique design, nationwide recognition for their walk-up stand was an impossibility.

With this simple aim in the forefront, professional architects in Southern California were approached. A few interesting concepts were drafted for the brothers' review, but unfortunately met with immediate rejection. Later described by Richard McDonald as "squatty looking" boxes, they exhibited a blatant lack of memorable charm or character.

Undaunted, the drawings were taken home for further contemplation. Then, while Richard McDonald pored over the plans in his office one rainy night, the arrow of inspiration found its mark. He had an idea. With limited talents as an artist but unbounded intuition about what a roadside stand should look like, he began to sketch some tentative plans.

First, the height of the building had to be lifted. Tapping into personal preferences, Richard penciled in a slanted roof, sloping gradually from the front to rear. Influenced by Colonial columns dominating his twenty-five-room house, he included a few variations. Though imposing, they weren't the elusive element he desired in a fast-food restaurant.

Next, he oriented a large semi-circle parallel to the front of the square building. It looked a little funny, so he discarded the idea and proceeded to draw two arches, positioning one of them at each side of the structure. This time, he arranged them perpendicular to where the road might be. As soon as he lifted his writing instrument from the paper at the bottom of the second arch, McDonald realized he had found the answer!

Swelled with the post-invention confidence typical of any vanguard, he presented Fontana architect Stanley Meston with the idea. Unprepared for the abstract incarnation of Coffee-Shop Modern, Stan posed his question: "Dick, did you have a bad dream last night?" The garish arches assaulted his design sensibilities! He wanted no part of them, detailing their obvious impracticality to the brothers. (Amazingly, he would lay claim to the arch idea—decades later.)

Unfazed by the response, McDonald stuck to his vision. He wanted those arches and would have them! If Meston wouldn't work with the idea, then they would get someone else. Predictably, Meston eventually caught the "vision" and cooperated with sign maker George Dexter to amplify the golden wings with neon.

After further refinements were made, an eye-grabbing rendering was drawn up. Now, curved circles became taught parabolas, flaring gradually at their base. The upper portions of the dual yellow bands, along with the edges of the flying wedge roof, were rimmed with tubes of neon. Walls, striped with dramatic red and white tiles, jazzed the exterior.

Businessman Neil Fox and associates took the hook and became the first McDonald's franchisee in America to construct the arched design. In May of 1953, the illuminated arches born on a scrap of paper finally came to life in Phoenix, Arizona. As they brightened the opening night with their futuristic energy, lines of customers were dazzled by the sight. To many, it was obvious that the age of the carhop was over. The amazing success story of Richard McDonald's golden arches was just beginning. ∎

© McDonald's System. Inc.

LOOK FOR THE GOLDEN ARCHES®

McDonald's

McDonald's Golden Arches
As the slogan went, "Look for the Golden Arches." Preziosi Postcards

McDonald's Golden Arch Building

According to Richard McDonald (co-founder of the original McDonald's chain), pilots in private planes flying during the 1950s reported that they routinely spied McDonald's neon arches from the air. When they were lost or disoriented, it was easy to find the airport; a McDonald's fast-food stand was almost always located nearby. Royal Photo Company Collection, Photographic Archives, University of Louisville

STAN'S SNEAKS ANOTHER ONE

*"Tumblers chilled in the deep freeze provided an icy reception
for extra-thick milkshakes—the kind you could actually
turn upside-down without spilling!"*

Stanley Burke's newest Fresno drive-in was pulling a sneak opening at 8 o'clock! Word spread quickly through the grapevine and within hours, the local network of cruisers mobilized to claim their share of the action. Around town, family sedans were appropriated from astonished parents as lead-sleds and flaming hot rods rumbled to action. Spilling from sidestreets onto the main drag, a phalanx of car customers convened on the virgin drive-in…simultaneously.

In the instant it took to slap the cheddar on a cheeseburger, the parking lot of Burke's newest eatery overflowed with chromed steel and lacquered

Stan's First Round Drive-In
Drive-in legend Stanley Burke was raised in a Cincinnati orphanage and came to Sacramento, California, during his teenage years. He started in the food business with money raised from odd jobs and purchased used equipment. In 1933, he opened a small shack on Stockton Boulevard across the street from a cannery. When he began selling beer, cannery workers made his place a regular stop. Beer suppliers, however, insisted he sold the brew too cold, a fact relished by the overheated workers. Eventually, Burke's small stand became a drive-in and the beginning of a chain. With a bank loan, his first circular unit was constructed on 16th and K Streets for a price of $20,000 in 1941. Its center spire, ribbed rooftop parapet, and Stan's sign were lined with neon tubing. Courtesy Martin Cable

sheet metal. Sixty minutes later, the grills were fired up for the first time as a legion of carhops sharpened their pencils in anticipation of the melee to come. As the inaugural patty of ground beef hit the hotplate, another circular construction of plate glass and neon tubing sizzled to life—the burger and shake at the very heart of its soul.

For ardent drive-in fans, the overwhelming crowd of cars present at that sneak opening in 1949 was no surprise. Burke's showy operation served what front-seat diners liked—within the privacy of their vehicles. His curbside canteens capitalized on two basic elements required for success: superior carhop service and lip-smacking food. Stan's circular creations set the standard for all California watering holes paying homage to car culture.

Immortalized in lights on Stan's streetside marquee, the quintessential image of a sprightly tray-girl set expectations high. Those drawn in by the fantasy weren't disappointed: Stan's hops were some of the best tray-toters working the West Coast. All nine of them talked the talk and walked the walk, creating the standard by which all others were judged. Rushing orders, substituting sides, or running for extra pickles—it didn't matter. Stan's girls knew how to treat customers like humans—earning tips with pleasing personalities and customer-is-always-right attitude.

But without the type of food that ensures repeat business no amount of carhop hospitality could create a loyal following. First and foremost, a drive-in had to have an appetizing menu—Stan's did. Based on the stacked creation popularized by burgermaster Bob Wian, Burke's crowd-pleasing "Double-Burger" possessed flavor characteristics all its own. All of the trimmings befitting the classic hamburger sandwich were stacked between the buns, including garden-fresh lettuce, tomatoes, pickles, and onions. There was no need for special sauce; freshness made the taste.

For dessert, mountains of home-made whipped cream were shot from specialized guns onto myriad fountain favorites. Oversized banana splits satisfied the most discerning customer. Tumblers chilled in the deep freeze provided an icy reception for extra-thick milkshakes—the kind you could actually turn upside-down without spilling!

Unfortunately, management problems and the shifting values of youth thawed the ice. One by one, the plug was pulled on the energetic neon of Stan's Drive-In restaurants. Today, most of Burke's circular structures have been demolished—victims of spiraling real estate values and the climate of cut-throat franchising. All of the carhops have long since retired, former burger flippers forced to take positions in coffee-shop kitchens. Nowadays, the roar of T-bucket hot rods and the laughing cackle of customers enjoying their food out in the parking lots up and down Highway 99 are but distant echoes.

Is the concept of the drive-in restaurant dead? Hardly! The sights, sounds, smells, and flavors that forged Stan's eateries into landmarks of memory live on in the minds of the California motorists lucky enough to have experienced

Stan's Circular At Night

Stanley Burke's first circular unit located at 16th and K Streets in Sacramento, California lit up the boulevard after dusk. During the 1940s, "Legs" the carhop was one of the main attractions, flashing her tray treats to motorists speeding past. Burke knew what the customer wanted and gave it to them. Circa 1941. H. Sweet Collection, City of Sacramento, History and Science Division, Sacramento Archives and Museum Collection Center

them. For anyone with wheels who has ever eaten at a carhop drive-in and fallen in love there, Stanley Burke's concept of the roadside eatery was—and always will be—the uncoronated king of automotive dining. Anyone who has ever taken a few loops "'round the Main" knows that. Long live the burger, the French fry, and carhop-service. Long live Stan's! ■

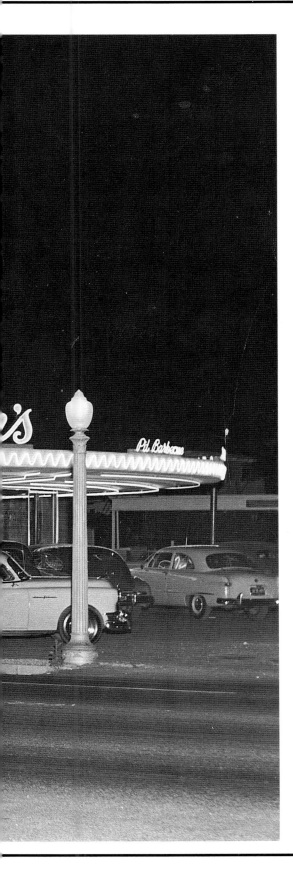

Stan's Carhop and Cadillac
Bakersfield Carhop Nita Howard was a favorite of car-customers at Stan's famous California eatery. Donning a snappy uniform reminiscent of the finest military service garb, she was a living, breathing icon of roadside service and a perfect example of the drive-in's friendliness, personal service, and the customer-is-always-right attitude. Courtesy Martin Cable

Stan's at Night
Left, the sign company that constructed the famous carhop neon for Stan's California Drive-Ins won an award for the effort. The colorful attention-grabber was inspired by "Legs," one of Stanley Burke's earliest carhops. Given free rein to take the essence of the curb server and immortalize her in neon, sign artisans created one of the most memorable marquees in drive-in history. This circa 1950s example once stationed at the Fresno Stan's is now a memory. Courtesy Martin Cable, Edwin Schober photographer

Sivils' Beauty Queen Pose Promo

Curb-girl Johnny McNeely poses at the left wearing another variation of the Sivils satin uniform. This version followed the lead of the more risqué cigarette girl oufits used at Sivils: satin shorts and a bare midriff top. The boots were custom-made, adorned with the Sivils name in leather. The young lady on the right is Margie Neal, one of those energetic cigarette sellers. Posing for this image wearing her tiara, she was fresh from an appearance in a local beauty contest. From the collections of the Texas/Dallas History and Archives Division, Dallas Public Library

Chesterfield Cigarette Girl

Opposite page, right, when Louise and husband J. D. Sivils opened their historic "drive-inn" restaurant in Houston, Texas, "curb-girls" were outfitted with colorful majorette uniforms made of satin. Louise Sivils explained that the idea for eye-catching service garb came to her after she saw this Chesterfield cigarette ad in the late 1930s. After Life magazine featured an article on the Sivils curb-girls in 1940, the majority of American drive-ins joined the stylized uniform parade. Before too long, carhops donning pert pillbox hats, satin jackets, short skirts, and polished boots were a common sight along the American roadway. Courtesy Liggett & Myers Tobacco Company

Decked Out Sivils' Carhop

Opposite page, far right, Louise Sivils came out with a new curb-girl outfit almost every year. Buna "Johnnie" Van Hekken models one of the classic satin majorette-type designs in this circa 1940s publicity photograph. This particular entry was made of bright red satin, trimmed with white sleeves and piping. The plumed hat followed the same color scheme, all the way to the white-feathered crest. Johnnie worked the south side cash register (the drive-in had two curb service ends) at the Houston location, taking care of inside customers with a style equal to the outdoor curb servers. From the collections of the Texas/Dallas History and Archives Division, Dallas Public Library

continued from page 89

ter's stands to an entirely new extreme, she legitimized the car service restaurant nationwide for anyone and everyone who owned a car. With white satin majorette gear featuring fringed epaulets, a plumed hat, decorative wrist cuffs, cowboy boots, and all the gold braid and piping possible, she stood proudly with her tray carefully balanced on one hand—while walking a full gait! When it came to satisfying hunger on the go, she became the nation's ideal curb-girl: rosy-cheeked, well-dressed, and just as polite. The girl next door with a Texas smile (and drawl to match), she was about as American as apple pie can get.

Both J. D. and Louise Sivils came from families with experience in the restaurant business. When they married in the thirties, they continued the family tradition by opening a restaurant of their own in Houston. It was a typical sit-down eatery with interior service,

worlds apart from the myriad stands setting up shop on street corners and vacant lots all over the city. Despite the differences, Louise was taken by the proliferation of these streetside hamburger businesses and began to consider the possibilities. Her intuition told her that the future was going to be car service, if only a few changes were implemented. There had to be a way to combine the excitement of the stands with the more dignified amenities of sit-down dining.

Louise discussed these views with her husband, explaining her notion for creating a grand restaurant to serve motorists, incorporating all the convenience of curb quickness. She would call it a "drive-inn," promoting the double letter combination to pique the interest of the customer and to bring a little more class to the operation. When J. D. balked, she countered with the comment, "Well, that's what people will do there…drive in!" While on the surface it seemed like a simplistic idea, it was actually pure genius. Until that time, no car service operation had used the term in combination with their name.

The Sivils opened their first Drive-Inn on the outskirts of Houston in 1938 and showed the rest of the nation how to run a world-class dining park. The differences were evident almost immediately! For starters, Mrs. Sivils dismissed the term "carhop" as too undignified. Jumping up and down on running boards was not going to be the way her girls greeted customers. They would do it with style, grace, and dignity. At her roadside palace, the window waitresses would be referred to as "curb-girls." The new title demanded a first-class uniform treatment, and fortunately, Mrs. Sivils was prepared. She had already dreamed up the ultimate image for the carhop years ago, long before America's restaurants even thought of stylizing their carhops. Inspired by an advertising drawing depicting a Chesterfield cigarette girl, it was an idea available for the taking. Luckily, Louise Sivils saw the connection first, had the uniforms made up, and brought the fantasy to reality.

The *Life* magazine article of 1940 summed it all up with the headline: "Houston Drive-In Trade gets Girl Show with its Hamburgers." But, this was much more than journalistic hyperbole; Louise Sivils' curb-girls really did put on an extravaganza! At each shift change, what equated to a live floor show-on-a-parking-lot commenced like clockwork. Practiced until perfect, the girls leaving their assigned posts would file into the building as a new team of workers made their debut on the lot. To the beat of music blaring out over external loudspeakers, Sivils' girls fanned out like players in a musical revue. Neatly lined up at each side of the parking lot in shimmering rows, it was time for inspection. Only then were they released to serve cars.

Patrons watching from the five-hundred-space parking lot were thrilled with the flamboyant floor show! Not only were they getting an appetizing meal with the best service in town, but entertainment as well. Visitors soon arrived from all parts of the state to witness the spectacle and taste the trout sandwich.

With a new standard of service to live up to, drive-in restaurants throughout the United States adopted similar styles for their car girls. Endless variations in costumes and serving

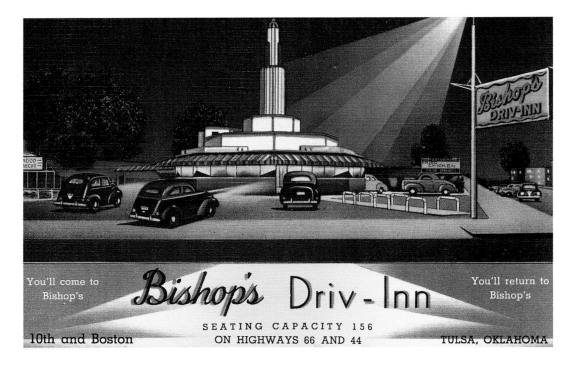

You'll come to Bishop's

Bishop's **Driv-Inn** **You'll return to Bishop's**

SEATING CAPACITY 156
10th and Boston ON HIGHWAYS 66 AND 44 TULSA, OKLAHOMA

Bishop's Drive-Inn
Above, octagonal design with massive pylon. Located on Highways 66 and 44 in Tulsa, Oklahoma, circa 1940s. Courtesy Chuck Sturm

Arctic Circle Drive-In Mascot
Left, "Acey" the chicken is the animal mascot used by the Arctic Circle drive-ins. From the Chuck Sturm Collection

styles proliferated. By the mid-forties, almost every motorized dining den in America featured some iteration of Louise Sivils' flashy satin garments. Even smaller drive-ins adopted the skirted style, including one modest operation located in San Bernardino, California, run by the two brothers named McDonald.

As more curbside restaurants became generally known as drive-ins, the carhop that started the legend in the early twenties with his athletic abilities and derring-do was replaced by the curb-girl. With running boards now fading to memory, the carhop became part service attendant and part showgirl. Undeniably, she was pure pizzazz—a dignified, hard-working gal gaining recognition as the undisputed queen bee of all America's drive-ins.

Now, the unparalleled act of eating in one's automobile was no longer a novelty in itself. It was a right shared by all those who owned an automobile. The actual restaurants that served those hungry folks sitting behind the wheel and riding in the backseat shifted into the spotlight. Now, the all-girl revue revolved around sparkling structures that lit up the night and set fire to the imagination. All

across the country, on busy intersections and along commercial approach routes, these beacons of light became the new focal point for captivated motorists.

The golden age of the American drive-in restaurant had begun. From here, it would only get better. New advancements were on the way to increase service and productivity—along with profits. Tired methods and inefficient processes would be abandoned for more reliable techniques. New advancements in food handling, refrigeration, and freezing would simplify preparation. The carhop would be aided by a new electrical device that could speed service and simplify tasks. Architectural embellishments would increase customer comfort. It all sounded promising as industry publications like *Drive-In Restaurant* and *Highway Cafe* debuted the latest ideas to come. Sure, conditions would improve, but from whose perspective? Only time would tell. ∎

SIVILS' HAMBURGER REVUE

"As imitators nationwide copied the style, legions of young women soon clamored for the available carhop jobs. It was an idea that appealed to many with sights set on careers in motion-pictures."

J. D. Sivils and his wife opened their first car service restaurant on the outskirts of Houston in 1938. They dubbed their operation a "drive-inn" and hired five "curly-haired cuties" to serve car patrons. With uniforms reminiscent of a Busby Berkeley musical, their satin-skirted carhops soon became the main attraction—much more appealing than the burgers, steaks, and trout sandwiches sold there.

While people in their cars waited for their food to be prepared, a small movie screen located on the rooftop provided further entertainment with cartoons and other featurettes. Automotive air-conditioning units with flexible hoses cooled vehicles and became a popular feature during the 100 degree days of summer.

A few years later a second restaurant was opened in the Dallas suburb of Oak Cliff, complete with north and south curb service and its own bevy of satin-clad beauties. A 500 car parking lot kept the girls busy: while curb servers hoofed it in boots, cigarette girls sped around on motor scooters. A "caller" positioned at the top of the building's central tower directed the gals quickly to new arrivals. As customers drove to their parking position, their precise location was relayed by intercom. Before the automobile stopped, a server was there, ready to take the order!

As imitators nationwide copied the style, legions of young women soon clamored for the available carhop jobs. It was an idea that appealed to many with sights set on careers in motion-pictures. In fact, winners of the state's top beauty pageants secured many of the Sivils' positions—some using their car-serve stint as a stepping stone to Hollywood. One-time Sivils' carhop Kay Williams did exactly that, taking her own shortcut to fame and fortune by marrying screen star Clark Gable.

However, it wasn't always all fun and glamour. Louise Sivils ran the Houston operation like a drill team. It was her responsibility to cull the best prospects from the applicants, eliminating all of those who weren't between the ages of eighteen and twenty-five from the running. To even be considered, carhop hopefuls had to be smart; high school diploma and health card were an absolute must. Even then, brains didn't insure employment. All of the Sivils' parking lot girls had to have good figures and exhibit "come hither" personalities to boot.

Mrs. Sivils ran a well-oiled production, often coaching the girls in speech and diction and why it was important to laugh at customers' jokes. More serious rules dealt with serving procedures, dictating that trays be balanced at ear level and held with one hand at all times. Touching the customer's car was not allowed and chewing gum while on duty was prohibited. Change had to be placed on the tray, not in the patron's hand. Actually entering a patron's vehicle was a mortal sin! A major rule infraction ended employment, a minor one resulted in punishment. Folding stacks of napkins often served as penance.

Sivils' Drive-In Card

At Sivils Drive In
Dallas, Texas

Sivils Dallas Drive-In
Life magazine's only drive-in cover girl was a Sivils curb-girl. Louise Sivils originated the idea of dressing curb-girls in satin shorts and majorette uniforms, beginning a trend that the rest of America's drive-ins would follow. When the

"caller" was perched high atop his central tower and the curb-girls were lined up at attention, Sivils Drive-In was a sight to see. In an age before theme parks, video games, and cyberspace, virtual reality was what one experienced from the front seat of an automobile. Preziosi Postcards

When the Oak Cliff area went dry in the late sixties and beer sales ended, Sivils' business began to decline. The usual reasons added to the demise: the busy intersection became too clogged for traffic flow, fast food stands offered quicker service, and customers changed. By then, a sinister box known as television provided more exciting imagery than a real drive-in ever could, frozen dinners wrapped within foil more convenience. By the time the Dallas landmark was closed, sold, and finally demolished in 1970, the nights at Sivils' seemed like a dream….

Satin shorts and shapely thighs…painted lips, golden hair, burgers and fries. Eyes peer out over a dash dappled with light—rows of motorists duplicate the sight. Look! Pillbox hats and majorette jackets, cigarette girls sell little white packets! Summer's first lightning bugs signal the call as lamps flash on and off, tires at rest. White boots on blacktop, numbers picked up, orders are served. Trays hook to windows—no papers, nor wrappers, real glassware, true style. Dollar bills go for food as smiles turn to laughs. Thanks very much. Did he tip? The smell of spilled beer and auto exhaust, songs for the feed blast out from the jukebox. Ya'll come back now! Oh, you racy Sivils carhop girls, how we wish we could. ∎

J. D. Sivils and his wife opened their first car service restaurant on the outskirts of Houston in 1938 with five "curly-haired cuties" to serve car patrons. With uniforms reminiscent of a Busby Berkeley musical, their satin-skirted carhops soon became the main attraction—much more appealing than the burgers, steaks, and trout sandwiches sold there.

Sivils' Cowboy and Uniformed Carhops
After Life magazine published an article about the Sivils' Drive-In location in Houston, Texas, shoulder patches embroidered with "Enjoy LIFE at Sivils" became part of the working outfit. During the forties, working as a Sivils curb-girl was considered by many young women to be the ultimate employment. Like the airline stewardess, toting trays to cars had a status all its own. The next best thing to being in show business, servicing hungry car-customers allowed many girls the chance to meet local celebrities, big-time movie stars, statesmen, and the occasional cowboy singer. From the collections of the Texas/Dallas History and Archives Division, Dallas Public Library

MEET ME AT THE VARSITY

*"By combining quality ingredients, friendly employees,
and assembly-line production, restaurant visionary Frank Gordy crystallized
his dreams of childhood into a world-famous landmark."*

When Frank Gordy was a small boy growing up in Thomaston, Georgia, most of his schoolmates fantasized about becoming baseball players, firemen, aviators, cowboys, or railroad engineers. At the turn of the century, those romantic careers were the standard stuff of children's dreams.

Yet, despite the worlds of fantasy these professions sparked in the imaginations of undeveloped minds, they held little interest for the enterprising Gordy. Even then, his sights were squarely set on owning his own business. Other aspirations paled in comparison. Throughout his schooling, he followed avenues compatible with his dream to bolster his original inspiration. After graduation from Oglethorpe University, shrewd investments coupled with the boom in Florida real estate paid-off. A nest-egg of $1,200 staked his first operation.

At age twenty-one, Gordy opened his first restaurant in Atlanta at the crossroads of Luckie Street and North Avenue in 1928. Christened the Yellow-

Jacket, it offered the collegiate crowd and passing motorists a convenient bill of fare. Soon after, Gordy wanted to expand his eatery's appeal to surrounding college communities, so a space large enough to serve extra customers was secured. The original moniker was dropped and the more general Varsity name adopted. Within a few years, the once-tiny hot-doggery had expanded to cover almost two city blocks.

Today, The Varsity Drive-In's food operation is unequaled, conducting business as the largest fast-food operation of its class on the entire planet. Every day of the week, a loyal following of Atlanta regulars descend upon the "V's" expansive ordering counter in hungry anticipation. In overall sales, the shear volume of automotive eats assembled, sold, and eaten staggers the imagination. On football Saturdays alone, 30,000 hungry Georgia-Tech fans jam the dining areas for their pre-game fill up. Even on the most routine days, well over two miles of hot dogs are gobbled up—along with 2,500 pounds of French fries, 5,000 fried pies, 7,000 hamburgers, and 300 gallons of chili! A torrent of Varsity Orange and chocolate milk flow freely, eclipsed only by enough Coca-Cola gallonage to float a battleship.

Prepared from the same tried-and-true family recipes Gordy perfected with his "million-dollar tastebuds," crispy fries are still made from the freshest potatoes—not frozen. Chili dogs, or "Heavy Weights" as they are known by customers, are world renowned for their flavor and imposing size. Fried to a golden hue and stuffed with flavorful filling, hand-pressed peach pies are a fitting showcase for Georgia's famous fruit. Of course, there's the hot and juicy "glorified steak" to consider, a fitting tribute to the institution of the American burger. Topped with lettuce, tomato, and mayo, it's the perfect companion to a piping hot order of batter-dipped onion rings.

Much to the customer's approval, the food served at The Varsity is only one small facet of its success. Out on the front lines, red-shirted employees never fail to greet customers with a smile and an excited, "What'll Ya Have?" The entire operation is galvanized by a spirit of cooperation and teamwork. Sandwich makers, burger flippers, hot dog cooks, singing curb-men—even members of the cleanup crew—are driven by one engine: pleasing the walk-up and drive-in diner with an unparalleled level of service and fabulous food.

By combining quality, friendliness, and assembly-line serving techniques, restaurant visionary Frank Gordy proved that even the most simplistic of childhood dreams can be worthwhile. Today, Atlanta's premier drive-in exists as an example of free enterprise at work, a living tribute to the man who once exclaimed, "The Varsity is my life and I love it!"

So, the next time you're in Georgia, motor on into the V and have them "walk a dog sideways" for you with a "bag of rags." Try a Mary Brown Steak or a Yellow Dog and be sure to ask about Flossie and his crazy hats. Check out the hot dog conveyor belt, have fun, eat well, and be sure to tell all of your friends. Frank Gordy would have wanted it that way. ∎

The Early Varsity
At age twenty-one in 1928, Frank Gordy opened his first restaurant in Atlanta at the crossroads of Luckie Street and North Avenue. Christened the Yellow-Jacket, it offered the collegiate crowd and passing motorists a convenient bill of fare. Today, his dream has expanded to become the world's largest drive-in eatery. Approaching motorists, pedestrians, and bus riders can smell the food from blocks away! Photo circa 1930. Courtesy of The Varsity, Inc.

Forties Varsity from Above
Atlanta's Varsity Drive-In has always provided numerous places to park. Two double canopies create ample shade during the hot summers and protection from the elements in the winter. With the amount of cars requesting food, it's enough to keep even the best curb-men busy. Courtesy of The Varsity, Inc.

The Varsity Park Lot, circa 1950s
Unlike the majority of drive-ins that chose to employ female carhops, the tradition at The Varsity has favored "curb-men." Nipsy Russell worked as an energetic server (he was number 46) years ago, long before his rhyming rise to notoriety on television and film. Flossie (another curb service veteran), gained his notoriety by singing the menu to customers! Courtesy of The Varsity, Inc.

Sixties Varsity and Street Scene
The Varsity is a patchwork of curb service spaces, awnings, and asphalt surrounding the famous fast food Mecca. Five television viewing rooms, inside seating for over 800 customers, and a continuously moving conveyor belt are only a few of the wonders. Inside, a 150ft stainless steel ordering counter is manned by dozens of employees, all eager to ask "What'll Ya Have," making sure you get your order quick. Courtesy of The Varsity, Inc.

THE TROUBLE WITH FRENCH FRIES

Served as a chip with clam dip, the sliced potato is classified by law as a fruit. When it accompanies a cut of steak, it suddenly becomes a vegetable. So, what happens when the starchy tuber is cut into small strips, fried in a vat of boiling oil, showered with salt, and teamed with a patty of chopped beef? Quite simply, the ordinary potato is transformed into a bag of French fries—a fast food drive-in meal maintaining a class all by itself.

French fries exist today as the perfect motoring finger food. Their size, shape, and packaging make them ideal for quick, easy consumption within the automobile. Indeed, they can be said to promote deep psychological satisfaction as well, for the very act of devouring them constitutes a re-enactment of behavior long forgotten, of times when our ancestors enjoyed dining without the benefit of "modern" utensils.

Despite this undeniable link to the past, French-fried potato sticks started life in America as an uninspired foodstuff, a plate filler to be chomped down between bites of burger and sips of soda. When the enterprising McDonald brothers finally began to lavish them with the attention they deserved during the forties, the once greasy potato strips at long last began their slow rise to the top of the fry basket.

For the McDonalds team, only the best Idaho Russets would do justice to this fast food side-order. Stored in small wire-mesh bins at the back of their warehouse, continuously circulating air moved among the containers, slowly aging the potatoes in the dry air of California. Only when they reached the peak of perfection were they ready to be peeled.

By the quarter sack full, the fry man tumbled potatoes into the hopper of a mechanized potato peeler. As an 18-inch abrasive wheel spun around, the spuds ambled about in every direction, efficiently stripped of their coverings. With just the right timing, they would emerge flecked with traces of skin, affording the most flavorful and visually pleasing fries in the free world. If left in too long, a robust bunch of potatoes were reduced to what Richard McDonald described as a handful of "little marbles."

As sack upon sack of potatoes were peeled and processed, the accumulated starch began its slow buildup. Eventually, it started overflowing from a drain vent pipe on the roof top! Using their proven "trial and error method" for finding solutions, the McDonalds hit upon the idea of eliminating the pesky starch with a soak in ice water.

Lucky for the customer, the age-old problems addressing taste were also rectified. Unlike many unscrupulous operators who used the same oil they deep-fried their fish and chicken in, Richard and Maurice decided at the start to use only the best, unadulterated cooking oil. When the French fries emerged—spattering all golden brown and a-burstin' with flavor—patrons begged for more.

Packed with labor and love, the three-ounce sacks of French fries sold for only ten cents—truly a rare bargain! Car customers were quick to recognize the value available at the McDonald's French fry window and soon it became the busiest portal for food in all of San Bernardino. Hundreds of future aficionados of the French fry lined up to order the crispy delights, readily acquainting themselves with the oversized aluminum salt shaker supplied at the walk-up serving window.

Today, it can be said that a little bag of French fries built an empire. After all, they were precisely what folks in a hurry wanted—a quick, hot, and cheap food, a fried variation of the ordinary potato that the McDonald brothers had lifted from its humble beginnings to a recognized form of American road food. ∎

First In French Fries
Circa 1950s advertising postcard from McDonald's depicting the candy-striped golden arches building.
Courtesy Chuck Sturm

Chrome And Fries
French fries have become the modern-day staple for the hurried motorist. New Haven, Connecticut

Plate of French Fries
Preziosi Postcards

NEWER VISIONS FOR ROADFOOD

Carhop Under The Canopy

Opposite, the 1960s brought unforeseen changes to the Wichita drive-in market. Griff's planned to locate four "fast-food" eateries in the area and Sandy's four of their own. To make matters worse, the McDonald's chain proposed construction of their own quartet. Kings-X drive-in owner Jimmie King took the incursion seriously, well aware that the sight of Golden Arches foretold an increased level of competition. Soon, overhead canopies and Western wear would not be enough to draw customers to his East Kellogg Street curb-server. A large Pontiac dealership now occupies the lot. Courtesy of Kings-X Inc.

Porky's Drive-In

Previous pages, the last of the famous Porky's Drive-Ins that once ruled Minneapolis and St. Paul. Founder and owner Ray Truelson began in the 1940s with the Adobe root beer stand situated at Hiawatha and 35th in Minneapolis. Around 1950, he opened the Flat Top Drive-In at 58th and Lyndale with a full line of drinks and food. The Flat Top was soon renamed Porky's, and a second Porky's was built in 1953 on Univeristy Avenue in St. Paul. Two additional Porky's were added in the late fifties at opposite ends of Minneapolis' Lake Street. The pictured Porky's in St. Paul closed its drive-thru window in 1979 and remained derelict throughout the 1980s, as did many of America's drive-ins. Faced with an ultimatum from the city to renovate or demolish, Truelson restored Porky's to its former glory in 1990. Today, the parking lot is packed with classic cars and hot rods on most summer nights, a flashback in time to the days when the classic drive-in first turned on its porcine neon sign. Michael Dregni

At the close of the 1940s, Richard and Maurice McDonald began formulating some innovative ideas to improve drive-in service. Although their San Bernardino, California, operation was lucrative, they perceived some basic flaws in the system and wanted to eliminate them. With an eye towards efficiency, they began an in-depth examination of their drive-in's strengths and weaknesses.

First, they noticed that postwar patrons were growing increasingly restless with carhop service. It wasn't anything obvious; only a feeling that car-diners wanted something more convenient. Richard McDonald observed that "the customer would come in and the carhop would go out. She would give them a menu, and go back into the drive-in again. When she returned, the customer might not be ready to make an order and she'd probably go back and forth four or five more times. Sometimes it was taking twenty-five to thirty minutes before people actually got their food served!" A service speed once considered an acceptable norm became noticeably sluggish.

Besides the sometimes slow rate of delivery, carhops posed other problems as well. Boyfriends regularly stopped by for prolonged chats, diverting them from their work. Because of the stand's proximity to a local high school, there was never a lack of eager males vying for attention. Every weekend, they descended upon the parking lot with their hopped-up roadsters and jalopies. The hours after dusk were filled with loud bragging, flirting, and the usual displays of male bravado that accompany adolescent mating rituals. Even more disturbing, carhops often quit at a moment's notice, leaving the McDonald brothers short of staff and long on disgruntled motorists blowing horns for service.

In perspective, most of these situations could be worked around when the occasion called for it. But what couldn't be justified was the monetary loss due to missing trays and

THE WORLD'S FAIR CORNUCOPIA

Despite the mysterious parentage of the ice cream cone, most historians agree on its birthplace: the St. Louis World's Fair. Although Italo Marchiony's patent on a split-cone mold was applied for prior to this event, he did not achieve the distinction of introducing the hand-held holder to the public. That achievement was shared among a group of vendors who were working the exposition in 1904.

That year, over fifty ice cream booths and waffle shops were operating within the sprawling fair grounds. Among the roster of concessionaires, three individuals staked their claim as original instigator of the consumable ice cream cone. While logic indicates that all three may have stumbled upon the concept simultaneously, subsequent obituaries and accounts in print claim otherwise.

Abe Doumar (Albert Doumar's uncle), now recognized by the Smithsonian Institution as the most likely originator, was employed by the City of Jerusalem Show during the day. After closing, he gathered with friends at a nearby waffle shop to chat. As crowds thinned, he got the notion to roll up a French waffle into an inverted spire. After filling it with a scoop of ice cream from next door, he suggested the waffle vendor sell the unusual combo to increase sales. To show his appreciation for the crowds, the ecstatic waffler presented Abe with one of his prized irons at season's end.

Another account relates how Ernest Hamwi sold Persian pastries from his concession stand. Baked on a flat waffle iron, he topped the latticed "zalabia" with sugar and other sweet toppings. When a nearby ice cream seller exhausted his supply of clean dishes, the inventive Hamwi rushed to his aid. Within seconds, a rolled up wafer became the receptacle for a dollop of frozen delight. The "World's Fair Cornucopia" made its momentous debut.

The last third in the infamous trilogy of cone creators was fair vendor David Avayou. As an observant visitor from Turkey, he claimed to have imported the ice cream cone idea from France, where he witnessed small frozen confections served in pointed paper receptacles. He applied the concept to his own wares and soon created an edible version to hold his frosty desserts.

Despite these conflicting origins, the popularity of the cone quickly gained momentum. Before the close of the Fair, several local foundries were scrambling to produce baking molds for the World's Fair Cornucopia. Eventually, everyone who had a hand in the development of the cone went on to profit from its meteoric rise to fame.

By the thirties, competition among cone manufacturers intensified, each attempting to outsmart the other with innovation. Marvels of edible engineering, "Dripless" models featured elaborate trough systems to trap melt. Others sported clever side-pockets for extra scoops. Exaggerated versions assumed the shape of spirals, space ships, and bathtubs.

As the cone became less of a novelty, the aggressive competition among manufacturers began to wane. Major bakeries began to dominate the field, eliminating creative offerings with functional cones. Soon, uncomplicated cake and sugar models triumphed. No longer a culinary work of art, the World's Fair Cornucopia was reduced to the status of ancillary food item with simple utility.

Eventually, the waffle-making legends of Doumar, Hamwi, and Avayou were forgotten. The ice cream cone became a separate entity, whole-heartedly accepted into the fold of American confections. Cones, and the frozen dessert they held, were now part of roadside food. ■

George Doumar and Waffle Maker
All the Doumar children learn to make cones when they are sixteen. Young George Doumar (shown here at age sixteen in 1983) represents the next generation of ice cream cone makers. Once learned, it's an easy process: Pull one of the four irons out on their tracks, open it, and ladle on a couple of ounces of batter. The filled griddle is slid over the gas flame and allowed to bake. Up and down the flame, the process is repeated, the irons flipped midway through the cooking process. As the first waffle becomes ready, the iron is pulled out, the top lifted, and the soft waffle wrapped around a tapered form made of wood. Then, the completed cone is placed into a cooling rack. Courtesy of Albert Doumar

flatware. Everyday, a plate or a knife or a fork would somehow leave the parking lot, never to be seen again. The dishes that escaped pilferage were dropped, lost, or accidentally thrown in the trash. Replacements were constantly cycled in from stock, only to be replaced again the following month. While the loss didn't bankrupt the business, it contributed to overhead costs. With a frugal New England ethic for thrift, the McDonalds couldn't tolerate the waste.

In the fall of 1948, they shut down the octagonal drive-in at Fourteenth and E Streets for three complete months. It was time to reshape the drive-in formula into a totally new entity, one that would operate on speed, efficiency, and self-service. The first order of business was the immediate dismissal of all twenty carhops. Next, windows used for pick-up were converted to self-serve portals where customers could place food orders. Then, the entire kitchen facility was gutted and reworked to accommodate two custom six-foot grills. Finally, the remaining stock of china, forks, knives, and spoons was phased out. From now on, edibles would be served in paper wrappers and soft drinks in disposable cups. This made the dishwasher's job redundant, so he was sacked, too.

The final stages included an entire rework of the menu. Because receipts showed that 80 percent of sales was from hamburgers, the hickory chip barbecue pit was dumped. The advertising money used to promote barbecue on the radio could now be saved. But there were even more changes to come: the twenty-five food selections currently offered were decimated to nine. The abbreviated menu was planned solely around hamburgers and cheeseburgers—all prepared the same way with ketchup, mustard, onion, and two pickles!

continued on page 116

It was time to reshape the drive-in formula into a totally new entity, one that would operate on speed, efficiency, and self-service. The first order of business was the immediate dismissal of all twenty carhops. Next, windows used for pick-up were converted to self-serve portals where customers could place their own food orders.

McDonald's After the Carhops Were Fired
In the fall of 1948, the McDonald brothers closed down their San Bernardino drive-in and fired all of the carhops. A new plan based on what they called the "Speedy Service System" was implemented. Its main features were self-service, minimal choice, and fast turnover. The 15¢ hamburger stand was born.
Courtesy Richard McDonald

DOLORES DRIVE-IN HOLLYWOOD

*"Screenwriters, producers, agents, stuntmen—
everyone involved with the creation of American celluloid—
would take their meals beneath the neon lights."*

Martin Cable had trouble finding a job when he returned home from the Marine Corps in 1946. Fortunately, drive-in dining spots occupied almost every street corner in Los Angeles, providing numerous opportunities for employment. When he heard that Ralph and Amanda Stephens were opening their second eatery at Wilshire and La Cienega and that they needed new carhops, his interest piqued. With only three dollars in his pocket, Cable hoofed it double-time over to Beverly Hills to join up.

His timing was perfect. That year, the male carhop crew working at the first Dolores location on Sunset Strip garnered a rather dubious reputation. Hiring strapping soldiers fresh from the military ranks was thought to be the perfect solution for upgrading the image. As a result, Cable was hired on the spot. There was only one obstacle: a white shirt, black bow-tie, and brown slacks had to be provided by the applicant. Cable's current wardrobe included only the green slacks he was wearing.

That night, he purchased a small box of dye for one buck and picked up a cheap bow-tie for another. He returned home and proceeded to dye his military trousers brown while wondering just how he would fare as a parking-lot waiter. By the close of the next day, his worries disappeared with his last car customer. A full shift of carhopping left his pockets bulging with tips and stained with dye! Wearing a grin wider than two slices of apple pie, he went home and confidently told his wife "not to worry…we've got it made!"

Four months later, Cable assumed the role of manager and began his drive-in education. From the outer parking lot to the kitchen, there was a lot to learn. First, he discovered that Amanda Stephens was an accomplished chef. She showed by example how important it was to have tasty recipes, illustrating the point with her famous onion soup and homemade pies. Under her wing, Cable found out just how much time and labor a profitable drive-in restaurant involved.

Making some discoveries of his own, Cable realized that ex-service folk weren't always the best candidates for outdoor food work. Aspiring actors fit the bill more appropriately and were soon applying for the jobs. As employee turnover changed the faces each year, he began noticing that some former hops were returning in snazzy cars. Having found fame and fortune in pictures, they returned to their old alma mater to hang out and flaunt their accomplishments on the silver screen.

Eventually, every movie actor or actress that came out to the Golden State got the tip to drive down to Dolores, and "try the pecan pie." The Beverly Hills location soon became a local landmark, the place to see—and be seen. During its heyday in the late forties, it became the restaurant of choice for the image-conscious Hollywood crowd. Screenwriters, producers, agents, stuntmen—everyone involved with the creation of American celluloid—would take their meals beneath the neon lights. The unassuming act of eating a hamburger often became an impromptu publicity event.

Gregory Peck was one of Dolores' best customers, as were many stars who drove in for a bite on their way to and from the studios. To avoid the prying eyes of gossip columnists, Tyrone Power rubbed fenders with Linda Christian in the most remote region of the lot. Vivian Leigh and her husband, Robert Walker, were also regulars. Susan Hayward motored in for car service often. Even character actor Ward Bond stopped in daily for hot coffee.

The expansive parking area beneath the striped awnings became the asphalt stage for displaying Hollywood's portable symbol of wealth: the automobile. Where else could a rising film star properly show off his or her luxury Packard or two-tone convertible? Cable recalls the day Bing Crosby stopped in to have his afternoon salad and flaunt his newest eight-cylinder acquisition. "Marty, guess what…just bought me a new Cadillac for $5500," he crooned. Despite the trappings of wealth and fame, Crosby's face revealed a man pained by the price. In those days, that could buy a lot of burgers! ■

Dolores Drive-In Wilshire
When the carhops at California's Dolores Drive-In were handed a dime for their tip, they tossed the coin on top of the roof in disgust. For some, this proved a lucrative habit. When times were tough during the winter months, it wasn't unusual to see one of the capped car servers scrambling atop the building, scouring the roof for some extra pocket money! During the heyday of the drive-ins, dining out in a motorcar meant only one thing: Dolores. This drive-in was the Wilshire and West La Cienega location, circa 1956. Bison Archives

Franchising Speedy Service
An executive from Southern California Edison and the brothers Richard (right) and Mac (center) McDonald discuss a new neon sign for their revamped drive-in. Richard specialized in marketing while Mac headed up operations. Courtesy Richard McDonald

continued from page 113

Meat patties were made smaller; now they would be ten to the pound instead of eight. This allowed for a "minor" price reduction and the usual thirty-cent sandwich swooped down to a low fifteen! The extra money saved by customers could be spent on three types of soft drinks, coffee, milk, fries, or a thick milkshake. The McDonalds' plan to create a volume operation through speedy preparation and self-service was ready for the ultimate test: the fickle public.

In December, the new walk-up stand reopened to a rather lackluster reception. From the start, the McDonalds' improved "Speedy Service System" didn't produce the volume anticipated. The customers hated it! They wanted the carhops back, they wanted the car service, they wanted the barbecue pit, they wanted the big menu. The once-bustling parking lot was reduced to three cars—and two of those belonged to employees! In the meantime, former carhops heckled, "We have our uniforms all ready—just call us!"

Apparently, the McDonalds changed the image of their stand too much. "We thought this was really going to knock 'em loose," recalls Richard McDonald. "Well, the only ones that it knocked loose were the McDonald brothers." Doubting the makeover, Maurice "Mac" McDonald said, "You know Dick…this looks like a dumb idea. What do you think…should we write this off and call back the carhops?" Although their pride was hurt, they decided to tough it out for a few more months. Three months later, their patience proved a profitable virtue.

Slowly, a more diverse segment of the market began showing up at the self-serve windows: taxi drivers, construction workers, salesmen, and motorists on their way to and from work. As the hangout image waned, even families began to frequent the stand. Small children soon joined in the melee, placing their orders independently as parents looked on proudly from the Buick.

During busy periods, lines were twenty deep at each service window. Inside, a crack assembly line of workers cranked out the food. With spotless stainless steel as backdrop, a "grill man" prepared the hamburgers, a dedicated "shake man" mixed up the milkshakes, and a separate "fry man" prepared the potatoes. "Dressers" added toppings and assembled the burgers, while the front "countermen" specifically concentrated on their tasks, wrapping food and taking care of customers. What was once an impromptu enterprise was now a smooth-running machine. The Speedy Service System worked!

News of the McDonalds' prototype spread fast and within the year, curious drive-in proprietors traveled from all over the country to see what made the unit work. The brothers

continued on page 120

DRIVE-INS ACROSS AMERICA

The Tik-Tok Restaurant
Left, the Tik-Tok was one of Portland, Oregon's, premier restaurants during the forties. While teenagers generally hung out at Bart's, a slightly older clientele sipped coffee at the Tik-Tok. Today, a parking lot occupies the former site. Oregon Historical Society

Yaw's Long Drive-In
Below, teenagers in Portland, Oregon, followed a complete "circuit" when they cruised during the fifties. First it was the Speck, followed by a trip downtown on Broadway. Coming back on the other side of town, Yaw's Drive-In became the next destination, along with 82nd Street. Back then, numerous curb service eateries jammed the strip. A McDonald's fast food outlet now occupies the site once designated to Yaw's. Oregon Historical Society

54 Drive-Inn Cafe
Left, today, the Highway 54 that passes through Kansas is nothing like the one that played host to drive-ins like the "54." The Kansas Turnpike now shoulders much of the traffic, along with the multi-laned interstate. Time and progress have passed by many of the old haunts…but fortunately, some may still be discovered. Courtesy Chuck Sturm

Harry Lewis Triple XXX
Below, Triple XXX Root Beer was a popular brand that assumed high visibility during the thirties and forties. Many of the drive-ins that sold the drink incorporated a root beer barrel into their design. Harry Lewis operated one such stand in Waco, Texas, featuring famous foods that garnered the approval of Duncan Hines. For early restaurateurs, earning the Duncan Hines seal of approval equated to guaranteed success. Hines started out in the restaurant review business by a fortunate stroke of fate. A well-traveled salesman, he had compiled a list of favorite eateries for his friends and family. The public's interest prompted Hines to expand the list and publish it as a book, entitled Adventures in Good Eating. By 1939, it was selling at a steady clip of 100,000 per year! Courtesy Chuck Sturm

Tiny Naylors

Above, William Wallace "Tiny" Naylor (he weighed 320lb at 6ft, 4in tall) started in the restaurant business around 1927. Waffle shops were his first foray into the world of roadside food. He slept in his first unit at night, alternating with a partner a schedule of rest and sleep. The single store grew into a chain of twenty-one, pleasing customers from Redding to San Diego, California. By 1949, he opened a Hollywood drive-in called Tiny Naylors and made his mark in the curb server walk-of-fame. On opening night, Humphrey Bogart commented that it looked like "a huge bird about to take off." That it did, satisfying customers with carhops on roller skates (for a few years) and copper heating pipes in the canopy. Despite protests, it closed in 1984 and was later demolished. Courtesy Dick Whittington Collection Dept. of Special Collections, University of Southern California Library

Merle's Drive-In & Barbecue

Left, the barbecue pit at Merle's was always fired and fried chicken was at the ready. Courtesy Chuck Sturm

continued from page 116

proudly revealed the entire operation, generously sharing the fast-food know-how they had developed. The intricacies of the stand were ravenously assimilated by all, and soon a number of similar burger bars popped up all across America. The McDonald brothers were definitely on to something big.

When a representative for Prince Castle Sales Division named Ray Kroc noticed that the McDonalds ordered more Multimixers than any of his other clients, he became curious. Why would anyone need ten of these multi-spindle mixers? More important, how could they possibly use all those machines at one time? During a sales trip in 1954, the puzzled Kroc decided to pay the San Bernardino hamburger stand a little visit.

What Kroc found captivated him. He couldn't believe the hundreds of customers driving up for hamburgers and was astonished at the lines. At first sight, he knew this busy operation had all the elements of great success—and he wanted to become part of it. The opportunity presented itself shortly: the McDonald brothers (who had already begun

World's First Fly-in-Drive-In
Below, Elwood, Indiana, was the town where Ruth and Charles Sullivan opened the world's first "Fly-in" drive-in. Known from coast to coast and located on Highways 13 and 37, it was a popular stopover for flyers looking for a quick lunch served in the cockpit. Preziosi Postcards

WORLD'S FIRST
Fly-In - Drive-In
ELWOOD, INDIANA

SULLIVAN'S

Track Service Drive-In
One of the most progressive enhancements to drive-in service was the "Motormat." Making its debut in 1949, this Los Angeles innovation promised the total elimination of carhops. At a new drive-in called "The Track," it attracted customers from as far as Santa Monica with its unique mode of service. Like horses at a watering trough, cars ringed around a central building, forming a circular pattern. Food rode the rails within carrying bins. Interestingly enough, each compartment was assigned its own name, much like horses at a real racetrack. "Ponder" is the unit depicted. National Archives

Sanders Court and Cafe

In Corbin, Kentucky, "Colonel" Harland Sanders got his start in the chicken business with a motel court he owned and operated during the forties and fifties. When a highway bypass around his original roadside restaurant caused business to plummet in 1955, he began selling his secret recipe chicken wherever he could. Kentucky Fried Chicken eventually became one of the giants in the fast-food industry. Unfortunately, mass-production methods made it impossible to re-create his tasty gravy. Courtesy Chuck Sturm

Multicolored Metal Drive-In Canopy

Lower right, in 1931, what is believed to be America's first drive-in canopy was installed at the Zangs Boulevard Pig Stand (Number 2) in Dallas, Texas. A brown canvas affair, it was the simple predecessor of the elaborate constructions installed during the fifties. Top Hat Drive-In operator Troy Smith followed in 1953 by installing Oklahoma's first drive-in canopy. By the start of the sixties, the canopy of multicolored sheet metal or corrugated tin was a common sight along the roadsides. Courtesy Brian Butko

franchising the concept to operators out West) suddenly found themselves without a franchising agent. Kroc became the perfect candidate to fill the position and readily took over the duties. With new zeal, the job of transforming the McDonald's name and its streamline system into a household word was begun. "Fast food" was on its way to becoming a dominant force in roadside dining.

In the meantime, America's drive-in restaurants were holding their own. Despite the incursion of self-serve burger walk-ups and soft-serve ice cream stands (such as Dairy Queen and Tastee-Freez), they continued to satisfy the expanding pool of motorists swelling the roads. But realistically, this new competition could not be ignored. Drive-in proprietors recognized that they had to act swiftly to keep stride with these low-overhead operations. To ensure the popularity of carhop service into the 1950s, changes were in order. Like every other consumer entity interested in appearance, functionality, and profits, the dri-

Richard's Drive-In
Richard's Drive-In of Cambridge, Massachusetts, featured a large weather-shielding roof to protect its in-car diners circa 1957. Richard's promoted "Car-feteria" service at its East Coast and Midwest dining operations. Extrapolating the theme of the young boy holding a hamburger (originally developed by Robert Wian with the double-deck "Big Boy"), Richard's utilized a male and female duo of similarly dressed youngsters, each holding their own hamburger. Cambridge Historical Commission

THE STORY OF CARBONATED WATER

The Transcendent.

The Transcendent Puffer Fountain
The Transcendent was featured on page 108 of A. D. Puffer and Sons' 1889 catalog. This elaborate structure was sold at the height of the soda fountain's Golden Age. The marble exterior housed a tank of carbonated liquid encased in ice beneath the counter. On each side were spigots that dispensed chilled syrup. Initially, these were called "fountains," but later, the name came to imply the complete counter area where sodas and ice cream were served. However, the dispensing fountain is still located under the serving counter in most of today's establishments. Landauer Collection, New-York Historical Society

When English scientist Joseph Priestley charged a glass of water with carbonic acid gas in 1767, it barely made a fizz in the chemistry community. Unlike his more astounding discovery of oxygen, the curious creation was largely ignored, treated by peers as a laboratory oddity.

About forty years later, Yale University professor Benjamin Silliman began experimenting with the idea of marketing the bubbling waters. Stopper bottles held the liquid, and exclusive shops in New York City sold them to thirsty patrons. Later, Philip Physick tried his own luck at the carbonation game by blending in a secret mixture of minerals. Sold widely as a cure for obesity, it helped to accelerate public awareness and desire for effervescent beverages.

When young Englishman John Matthews arrived in New York in 1832, he saw this yearning for fizzy drinks as an opportunity for fortune. By exploiting his unique skill for producing carbonic acid gas, he almost singlehandedly popped the top on the soda water market. Incorporating his ideas into a portable, doghouse-sized carbonating apparatus, he revolutionized the soda water business with his practical "fountain."

Store owners were amazed by the new device, even if they did not understand the scientific principles that made it work: when proper proportions of sulfuric acid, carbonic acid, and water were filtered through marble dust, carbon dioxide gas was liberated. The resulting liquid became a modified sort of water—highly saturated with myriad harmless bubbles, all eager for simultaneous release.

As Matthews secured rights to gather the scrap marble (enough to carbonate 25 million gallons) from the construction site of St. Patrick's Cathedral, established manufacturers began to take notice. Soon, aggressive corporations like Boston's A.D. Puffer and Philadelphia's John Lippincott debuted elaborate versions of their own fountains.

In the competition to follow, an incongruous hodge podge of decorative styles soon found their way into new fountain designs. Ostentatious motifs were typified by bare-breasted nymphs, decorative orbs, beaded strings, and spear-toting centurions. Still, the era's drugstores and sweet shops adored the haughty designs and purchased them without restraint. Aficionados of American soda now had the freedom to order a tumbler of unadulterated seltzer water whenever and wherever they pleased.

At first, inhibited converts to the bubbly liquid imbibed it totally straight, slightly chilled. Fortunately, attitudes about additives began to soften when perfume dealer Eugène Roussel arrived in Philadelphia from France.

A short while after he opened a bustling perfume emporium, he began to offer the sparkling water to his clients. No stranger to experimentation, he put aside his fragrances and began dabbling with flavors around 1838. Like magnet to steel, soda and syrup joined and a tasty new drink sensation was born: the flavored soda.

Not surprisingly, the tingling taste treat was an immediate hit with the socializers of Philadelphia's soda parlour scene! Re-energized by news of the phenomenon, fountain operators city wide began the scramble to produce their own custom made beverages.

Within a few years, no reputable soda fountain would be caught without a vast stock of vanilla, cherry, pepsin, birch beer, kola, champagne, or claret flavored syrups under the counter. Tickling the taste buds and soothing the palate was the new domain of carbonated waters. ■

Leon's Custard
When you're in need of a frozen custard on a hot day, the last thing you want is to sup on your delicacy in the blazing sun. Canopies and overhanging roofs provided an oasis. In Milwaukee, Wisconsin, Leon's Custard Stand continues to outshine many of the other ice cream bars.
Courtesy Richard Schneider

The most progressive enhancement was the "Motormat," which debuted in 1949 in Los Angeles and promised the total elimination of carhops. Twenty semi-circular parking spaces bridged a center hub kitchen by means of metal tracks. Food and condiments rode the rails within carrying bins, each compartment powered by a small 1 1/2hp motor.

ve-in segment of the restaurant industry welcomed all improvements.

One of the most progressive enhancements was the "Motormat." Debuted in 1949, this Los Angeles innovation promised the total elimination of carhops. At a new drive-in called "The Track," it attracted customers from as far as Santa Monica with its unique mode of service. Like a group of horses at a watering trough, cars ringed around a central building, forming a circular pattern. Twenty semi-circular parking spaces bridged a center hub kitchen by means of metal tracks. Food and condiments rode the rails within carrying bins, each compartment powered by a small 1 1/2 horsepower motor.

The mechanical setup was reminiscent of the wackiest Rube Goldberg device. Positioned in a pre-determined parking space, the customer rolled down the car window and was greeted by a stainless-steel bin that could be pulled flush with the door. Inside the box were plastic cups, a water bottle, menu, order pad, and change tray. It was large, too. Food for six people could be ferried back and forth on the elevated platforms. Patrons would jot down their orders and with the push of a button, the unit scooted a return into the kitchen.

When the empty bin arrived at the kitchen, an attendant put through the order and added up the bill. As hamburgers and other entrees were prepared, the rail box made its second journey to the automobile to collect the money. By the time it returned to the preparation area, the food was ready to go—loaded into the compartment along with condiments and the customer's change. According to inventor Kenneth C. Purdy, the spoke-wheel-track arrangement sped service 20–25 percent. Best of all, it reduced labor costs, making the large staff of carhops normally required to run a drive-in unnecessary. And, there were benefits for the customer,

continued on page 128

AIR-COOLED COMFORT DINING

Drive-in restaurant dining often had distinct advantages. Automobile owners could enjoy the great outdoors while consuming their food—without the hassles of a roadside picnic. As the sun's rays shone through the front windshield, frosty milkshakes and steaming cheeseburgers could be eaten without a care.

Of course, this idyllic scene was only indicative of the milder times of year. Taking lunch at a curb-service restaurant during the summer months often posed discomfort. In extremely humid cities like Houston, Texas, the metal surfaces of an automobile often created an oven-like environment when heated by the sun. As more and more indoor eateries featured "air-cooled by

refrigeration," drive-in operators were literally left in the dust—and the hot air that held it.

Houston drive-in proprietor and visionary R. E. "Sonny" Stuart decided to fight fire with fire—or in this case hot air with cold—during the Texas summer of 1955. By employing the latest in modern technology, he offered his own version of air-conditioning to a public prostrated by the heat. America's "most air-conditioned city" became the proving grounds for a revolutionary new kind of drive-in climate control.

As the mysterious installation was in its last stages of completion, curious customers drove into Stuart's to see what all the rumors were about. Before they could engage their parking brake under the canopy, a smiling carhop greeted them with two flexible hoses in hand. To the uninitiated, it seemed like a scene from a science-fiction serial: tubes ribbed with accordion-like folds were thrust into the front vent window and instructions given to roll up all others. Just what was happening here?

Surprise quickly turned to delight as overheated passengers literally breathed a deep sigh of approval. As a refrigerated column of air began pouring into the vehicle's interior, interior metal cooled. By means of simple convection, hot air was forced out through the second exhaust tubing, jammed in above the first.

Suddenly, the temperature inside the automobile dropped! In the short time that it took for the car server to return with an order, the car became as cool as a mountain cabin. For the next fifteen minutes, drinking and dining was virtually perspiration-free. Parked side by side under the glowering heat island of the city, automobiles became miniature oasis for comfort dining.

A few feet above under the canopy, advanced air-conditioning facilitated the transformation. Designed and manufactured especially for this unique application, Stuart's refrigeration units were the first full-scale trial of practical drive-in air-conditioning. Since seventeen were installed, the project wasn't cheap: the specialized three-quarter ton coolers served two customers at a cost of almost $500 each!

Still, the investment proved worthwhile for the enterprising Stuart. After the installation, drive-in business increased over 20 percent. Customers that ordinarily just pulled in to buy a cold beverage were now requesting food. Since normal business averaged 1,000 cars per day at each of his two locations, it didn't take long to recoup startup costs.

As the last pieces of burger were swallowed, customers signaled to the carhop their readiness to leave. Tubings were removed from the window, retracted by long springs. Transformed like a Cinderella carriage, hot air replaced cold in one gulp. The refreshing trip to Sonny Stuart's amazing drive-in was over. ∎

Marquee Drive-In
Combining a circular layout with an overhead canopy parking area was a natural progression for drive-in restaurants operating in extreme climate conditions. Located at 216 East Main in Mesa, Arizona, the Marquee was a welcome watering hole when the summer temperatures edged over the century mark. Inside diners had it even better: "refrigerated" air cooled the overheated brow. Circa 1960. Courtesy Karl Korzeniewski

A smiling carhop would greet you with two flexible hoses in hand, which were thrust into the front vent window. As a refrigerated column of air began pouring into the vehicle's interior, interior metal cooled. By means of simple convection, hot air was forced out through the second exhaust tubing, jammed in above the first.

Drive-In Air Conditioning
Air conditioning was a novelty tried by many drive-in operators during the fifties. R. E. "Sonny" Stuart used the radical system at his Houston drive-in, as did J. D. and Louise Sivils.

The ultimate canopy was finally produced, which "served as flower gardens filled with color and life, but without the time-consuming necessity for taking care of flowers." It kept customers out of the rain, provided visual enjoyment, and replaced the natural flora of the American roadside. Who needed parks with grass and real trees? The drive-in had it all.

Canopy Styles
Council manufacturing of Fort Smith, Arkansas, introduced a wide range of canopy styles during the fifties and sixties. Forward-thinking operators could choose from models like the curved, lazy boomerang, pitched, canted, and folding plate. © 1994 Gabriele Witzel

continued from page 125
too: a large "No Tipping" sign hung on the building facade.

Despite its labor-saving features and promise of thrift, the impersonal track system never caught on. Even so, the frenzy for other mechanical contrivances continued. In Hammond, Indiana, the "Driv-O-Matic" Drive-In relied on a conveyor belt to deliver food out to its carhops. By using a continuous belt over 62 feet long, co-owner and inventor Mrs. Edwin Bennett side-stepped the need for girls to run "helter-skelter around the parking lot." When the food appeared at the end of the outgoing belt, the girls would deliver the trays to the appropriate vehicle and return the soiled dishes to the conveyor.

Eventually, systems like these were regarded as curiosities—unique, but certainly not a threat to conventional carhop service. During the early 1950s, the majority of car-dining patrons still preferred personal interaction with a carhop. It was an accepted form of service that had characterized the industry for over three decades. Like the lunch counter waitress and the service station attendant, she was an integral part of roadside culture that couldn't be replaced so easily. At first, the acceptance of minimal carhop service would be slow, but once the idea took root there would be no turning back.

As the consumers of American convenience foods continued to gulp milkshakes

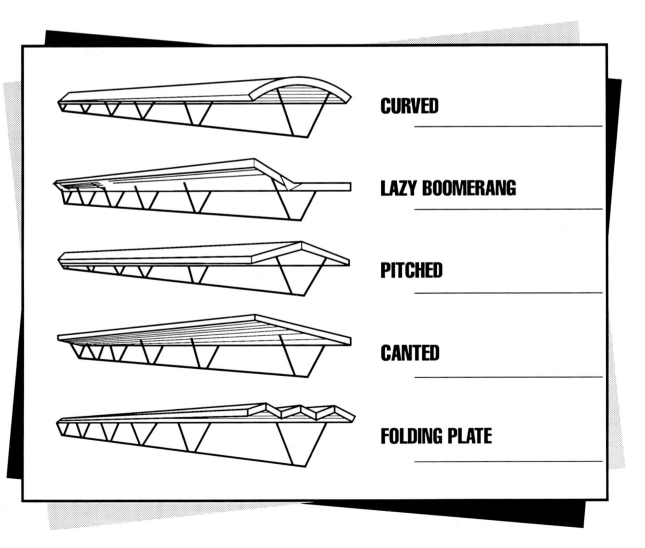

CURVED

LAZY BOOMERANG

PITCHED

CANTED

FOLDING PLATE

and cheeseburgers in the open-air dining rooms, the restaurant industry continued dreaming up new ways to attract customers and increase comfort. One method was the utilization of overhead canopies to provide an oasis of shade, particularly in the hot summer sun of the Southern and Southwestern states. In 1931, Dallas Pig Stand number 2 became America's first curb server to install an elevated canopy of brown canvas. Although business was good during morning hours, it diminished in the afternoon when the sun's heat permeated the parking lot. With this unique covering, the Pig Stand promoted business during the hottest hours, providing customers with luxurious shade.

Surprisingly, it took other drive-in operators almost thirty years to recognize the canopy! By the late fifties, interest picked up and most curb operations were installing some type of raised protection. With a minimal investment in time and materials, any modest refreshment shack could sport an updated appearance with the installation of a suspended overhead roof. The benefits were numerous: not only were canopies instrumental in providing customer comfort, they also improved employee morale. Now, carhops could enjoy the fringe benefit of working under protected coverings in a cool and dry comfort zone. Customers loved the shady parking lots and business improved.

As new materials were developed, the canopy matured. Canvas sheeting was soon replaced by lightweight nylon, laminated with vinyl. Ideal for use in harsh climates, this pliable fabric proved extremely colorfast, wear resistant, and durable. Next, flexible metal panels made their debut, providing manufacturers the perfect material to produce pre-fabricated canopies. Easily assembled on site, drive-in owners could now create stunning structures with minimal effort and investment.

Soon, the reasons for installing a canopy became more than just functional: they were a great decorative element and caught the at-

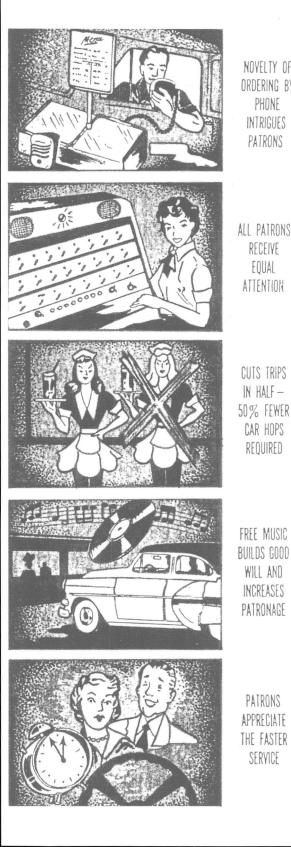

NOVELTY OF ORDERING BY PHONE INTRIGUES PATRONS

ALL PATRONS RECEIVE EQUAL ATTENTION

CUTS TRIPS IN HALF — 50% FEWER CAR HOPS REQUIRED

FREE MUSIC BUILDS GOOD WILL AND INCREASES PATRONAGE

PATRONS APPRECIATE THE FASTER SERVICE

As carhops were supplanted by vacuum tubes, the radically new format of car service inspired the slogan "Service With the Speed of Sound."

Order Phone Advantages
Remote ordering units at the drive-in offered many advantages—including the elimination of carhops. Motiograph, Inc., of Chicago manufactured the Servus-Fone, an advanced unit promising to "improve your service with half the help."

Teletray Ordering Unit
The Teletray electronic ordering system was a popular model used to speed ordering efficiency at the drive-in of the fifties. Unlike the belt-mounted ordering communicators used today, talking with customers within their cars often required a central operator manning a large, interior switchboard. National Archives

ing and falling plates running its entire length. But none could compare with the "Rock and Roll," a sine-wave copy that featured contrasting colors above and below its crests.

The so called "doodad frame" was another curious addition to the lineup with steel frames 6 by 4 feet, supporting a number of irregularly shaped pieces of metal tensioned by springs. As reported by *Drive-In* magazine in April of 1958, the doodad frames "served as flower gardens filled with color and life, but without the time-consuming necessity for taking care of flowers." The ultimate canopy was finally produced: one that kept customers out of the rain, provided visual enjoyment, and replaced the natural flora of the American roadside. Who needed parks with grass and real trees? The drive-in had it all.

Canopy aesthetics were soon overshadowed by a greater development. In 1955, Buddie's Food 'n Fun opened a new car service outpost in Brooklyn, New York. The gala event featured "Captain Video" who blasted off from the rocket ship "Galaxy" and handed out space cannons and other valuable prizes to the kids. It proved to be a timely promotion, since a number of manufacturers were already introducing futuristic communications equipment to a receptive drive-in market. That year, the Fone-A-Chef Company debuted a thoroughly modern intercom cast of aluminum and finished in "high luster automobile enamel." Borrowing the best features of Detroit's latest cars, Fone-A-Chef's new units featured gleaming tray-bars of chrome and high-fidelity speakers. Car service was entering a new stage.

This Space Age technology—with its promise to keep costs down, send sales soaring, and speed up service—probably originated during the onset of the fifties. More than likely, an enterprising drive-in theater operator got the notion to make his window speakers work both ways. Why not allow the customer to talk into the speaker head instead of just listening to it? With the addition of a few off-

tention of the motorist with the same ease as a large billboard. First implemented by the Illinois-based Dogs 'n Suds chain in 1953, the "Butterfly" canopy featured uplifted "wings" that served as visual magnets. Other assemblies like the "Flying Saucer," a gigantic 40-foot-diameter behemoth, incorporated both nylon sheeting and steel framing. With their grandiose attitude and sparkling colors, these structures were difficult for passing customers to ignore.

During the sixties, Ohio canopy manufacturer Selby Industries took these elaborate creations even further. Selby's "High 'n Hailing" model was the height of modernism: 20-foot parabolas stretched skyward above a flat overhead at intervals of 20 feet. Beneath the arcs, suspended geometrics provided decoration. The "Mountain Range" was a more subdued style, providing angular effects with rising and

the-shelf electrical components, food orders from the snack bar could now be taken directly from cars. At first, a minority of perceptive drive-in owners picked up on the innovation and began to install their own kitchen-based public address amplifiers. It didn't take long for the rest to follow.

When drive-in owner Troy N. Smith stopped at a Louisiana car joint for lunch in 1954, he encountered the cable talk-back system for the first time. He returned to Shawnee, Oklahoma, and enlisted the expertise of a local radio repairman to install one of the parking lot communication systems at his own drive-in. As carhops were supplanted by vacuum tubes, the Top Hat Drive-In became the first Oklahoma eatery to go totally elec

continued on page 136

Placing Order at a Speaker Box
The remote-order speaker box was an advancement that promised to improve the bottom line at America's drive-ins. While this may have been true for the operators, carhops didn't fare so well. As technology replaced footwork, curb-girls were relieved of their duties in large numbers.
National Archives

NOBODY HOPS LIKE SONIC

*"Electrified by the latest in modern gadgetry, curious teens
took to the inventive ordering devices and jumped at the chance to play
fast-food disc jockey within their vehicular cocoons."*

On the outskirts of Shawnee, Oklahoma, where North Harrison Road turns into Highway 18 and the neon turns to woods, Troy Smith purchased a small root beer stand in 1953. He liked the log house that came with the deal and figured he could utilize the soda pop business to finance his ultimate plans of building a family restaurant. In his mind, the cabin out back would become the real goldmine…once he converted it into a full-service eatery.

Smith borrowed the capital needed to improve the stand and wasted no time transforming it. He named it the Top Hat and installed Oklahoma's first drive-in canopies, visually upgrading the structure. Steel supports held the

Top Hat Aristocrat Hamburgers
The Dachshund dog was not only a symbol of the hot dog, but Troy Smith's early drive-in restaurant, the Top Hat. He opened the curb service restaurant during the early fifties and installed electronic speaker boxes to assist customer ordering. Sonic Drive-Ins originated from that first little stand. Courtesy Sonic Industries Inc.

wooden coverings aloft, offering car customers increased protection from the weather. Next, a series of neatly organized parking stalls were established to improve traffic flow and end congestion, one row on each side of the building. Finally, the shack was modified to allow carhops to pick up their food orders inside.

Convinced he could streamline the process of ordering food, Smith called on a television man to construct an electronic intercom system for the reorganized car lanes. Hot vacuum tubes, mechanical relays, clunky switches, carbon microphones, and thick wiring soon became part of a practical intercom system. Speaker housings much like those used at the drive-in theater contained the bulky components. Cables coiled from each communicator to an upright post. Each parking position had its own ordering unit, every customer a hand-held line to the kitchen. It was another historic first for Oklahoma car customers.

While the new ordering apparatus proved to perform flawlessly, Smith worried that the new technology might not be accepted. To calm his anxiety and ensure the success of his investment, he decided a catchy slogan was needed to generate excitement prior to grand opening. But how could he convey the ideas of speedy delivery and customer service with one simple phrase? He was confident his carhops could outdo the tray-boys at the A&W across town, but he was unsure how to express it. Suddenly, he realized his high-speed ordering boxes held the answer: "Service with the Speed of Sound!" Smith was ready to welcome the public.

Within a matter of weeks, the once inconspicuous root beer stand on the edge of town became the buzz of Shawnee's drive-in restaurant crowd. Suddenly, every curious citizen with a driver's license in their wallet and a gallon of gasoline in their automobile wanted to check out the town's newest carhop eatery. As the fledgling sounds of rock'n'roll tapped out a steady beat, a crowd of motorized youth queued up for the best parking positions. Families followed, station wagons brimming with children. Toddlers pressed inquisitive noses to the glass as their elders shook heads in disbelief. Just what was this futuristic setup?

Electrified by the latest in modern gadgetry, curious teens took to the inventive ordering devices and jumped at the chance to play fast food disc jockey within their vehicular cocoons. For a while, even the car radio took a backseat to the unique ordering gimmick. "Favorite station buttons" introduced by Detroit on the latest models were quickly ignored as the novel telephones were favored.

News of the excitement spread and Smith soon fielded inquiries from dozens of interested entrepreneurs. Former supermarket manager Charlie Pappe was one of the first, anxious to learn how the revolutionary operation worked. A partnership was formed and soon a second Top Hat opened. Two

Early Sonic Speed of Sound
During the late fifties, Sonic provided "Service With the Speed of Sound" to its drive-in customers. Signboards depicted all the energy of the atom and its idealized electrical discharge. Scientifically, it may not have been totally correct—although it was fanciful enough to sell hot hamburgers and onion rings. Basically a small rectangular building straddled by two canopies, the first Sonic outlets were simple affairs that offered tasty food. Every car stall had an ordering unit, each customer a "direct line" to the kitchen. Courtesy Sonic Industries Inc.

more units followed, as did plans to franchise the success of the expanding operation in 1959.

The drive-in business begun by Troy Smith with one root beer stand and an idea to speed up service was at the crossroads. Since "Top Hat" was already registered as a trademark, Smith checked the dictionary and discovered his catchy motto could be represented by just one word: Sonic. As America left the age of propellers and entered the jet age, the future of drive-in restaurants was secure. For the next three decades, automotive diners could—and would—get their "Service With the Speed of Sound!" ■

SONIC
America's Drive-In

MARCH SPECIAL
CHICKEN & TOTS
ONLY $2.79

Electrified by the latest in modern gadgetry, curious teens took to the inventive ordering devices and jumped at the chance to play fast food disc jockey within their vehicular cocoons. The high-speed ordering boxes were truly "Service with the Speed of Sound!"

Sonic Drive-In
By the time C. Stephen Lynn became President and Chief Executive Officer in 1983, Sonic's number had grown to over 900 units. When Lynn and key management completed a leveraged buyout in 1986, Smith's original philosophy that "owners make better managers" helped rocket the organization to prominence. By 1994, Sonic became America's number one drive-in with over 1,300 units in operation. At America's Sonic Drive-Ins, the window-mounted serving tray has been re-incarnated as a one-piece plastic model. The automotive machines of yesteryear sported windows made of flat glass; today, curved glass dictates that the tray mount "hooks" provide extra clearance to keep the tray rigid while installed. Stopping for a 'burger are Clare Patterson and his 1955 Chevrolet and Dan Daniels and his 1939 Cadillac at this East Central, Wichita, Kansas, location.

continued from page 131

tronic. The radically new format of car service
inspired the slogan "Service With the Speed
of Sound" and the name for a new chain. It
was the beginning of the Sonic Drive-Ins and a
new dimension in curbside service.

With its practicality proven, the rush to install electronic ordering networks was on.
From 1951 until the end of the fifties, a wide
assortment of models was introduced. All the
industry publications featured articles on the
two-ways, introducing the modern restauranteur to an engaging roster of brands with
names that exuded speed and convenience:
the Aut-O-Hop, Ordaphone, Fon-A-Chef,
Servus-Fone, Teletray, Dine-A-Mike, TelAuto-
graph, Dine-a-Com, Auto-Dine, and Electro-
Hop. Each boasted myriad features that included internally illuminated menus, record
changers, dual-speech amplifiers, an ability to
play music, and spring-mounted posts that
bounced back when hit by an automobile!

With the acceptance of the hard-wired
communications systems, surplus wireless
equipment found its way onto the asphalt,
too. Portable "walkie-talkies" proven during
World War II were soon utilized by drive-ins
looking for a memorable gimmick. Serving
customers on Kentucky's Dixie Highway,
Schilling's Drive-In chose the "Wireless Exped-
itor" for its carhop-to-kitchen communiqués.
Customers were impressed with the hand-held
devices toted to their cars and showed inter-

est by spending more money on hamburgers.

Milwaukee's Ace Foods followed the radio trend with portable, eight-pound transceivers of their own. Operating on a short-wave radio band and licensed by the Federal Communications Commission with their own call letters, three roving radio girls relayed food tickets from a 136-car lot to a central control dispatcher based in the kitchen. Over 950 customers could be served nightly with the shoulder-strap devices, with more efficiency than five carhops on the run. This was definitely the stuff science fiction was made of, well received by a public ravenous for images of the future and the latest in labor-saving devices. Now, customers had an instant way to make their requests known. The carhops had electronic allies—or did they?

Planning their strategy for the future, the owners of America's drive-ins had an ulterior motive: improve the bottom line. High labor costs, training, turnover, and other problems concerning employee relations were becoming more of a deterrent for using real, live waitresses. For many, it became evident that an inanimate machine offered a lot less trouble for a one-time investment. More important, radio speaker boxes were never late for work and didn't talk back when they were told to do something. Taking the lead followed by the McDonald brothers more than ten years earlier, drive-ins "upgraded" by methodically eliminating their surplus parking lot personnel.

By the 1960s, multiple trips back and forth to the automobile became a tired custom of the past. With the aid of electrical impulses, the curb-girl now had only one complete circuit to make: one trip to deliver the food and drinks, the other to retrieve a tray full of dishes…and her tip.

During the extra time freed up by the speedy ordering practice, the remaining curb-girls had pause to consider their pole-mounted helpers. Sure, intercoms made their work more efficient, but how long would it take be-

fore the last of the carhops were replaced? Those with any sense could see that the entire concept of the carhop was in danger. The unseen specter of remote menus and the drive-thru window were already being refined for tomorrow's restaurant designs.

What should have been a positive force for improvement slowly turned into a negative contribution to the drive-in's denigration. The once-elegant concept of bringing food and drink out to people parked curbside was being improved…right out of existence.

In the end, the advent of technological aids would prove to be the first nudge toward a more impersonal roadside. One particularly outspoken manager summed up the attitude in an industry magazine: "we don't have to take a lot of time selecting people with an education. If she can smile, if she can talk, and if she is nice, she doesn't have to be a salesman anymore…because we can do that from the switchboard." The quest for faster service, more customers, larger food sales, higher

continued on page 141

Only Aut-O-Hop Has AMG!
Intercom manufacturers employed every gimmick they could think of to sell their new units. Special circuitry, noise canceling microphones, and pre-recorded messages were the latest improvements. The carhop was suddenly outmoded—or was she?

Fone-A-Chef
Opposite, far left, the 1956 Fone-A-Chef was the future incarnate. As this magazine ad promised, "This revolutionary new 'service-in-seconds' electronic ordering and music system for Drive-Ins engineered by automation specialists and designed by Detroit automobile stylists, will send your sales soaring!"

AUTO RADIO ROCK 'N' ROLL

Electric Push-Button Tuning
Soon after there was a radio in every car, push-button tuning was invented to allow instant access to your favorite station.

Crosley Roamio Car Radio
Once the radio receiver became a permanent feature of the American motorcar, the public began to view the luxury as a basic right. When rock'n'roll music began energizing the airwaves during the fifties, there was no turning back—the car radio became a vital link to the car culture of youth. Living without one was tough.

With their 100-watt transmitter broadcasting returns of the Harding-Cox election of 1920, Pittsburgh's KDKA became America's first commercial radio station. Imitators soon followed, and within a couple of years, almost two-dozen stations were sending radio waves into the ether. By 1923, the kilocycle band became crowded: the number of licensed stations jumped from just sixty to 573!

As hooking radio transmissions from the sky became a popular pastime for home hobbyists, motorists became intrigued with the possibilities. Radio magazines anticipated the interest and began detailing do-it-yourself plans for mobile radio-receivers.

The Automobile Radio Corporation sidestepped the craze for kits with their "Transitone," designed to fit behind the instrument panel of almost any vehicle. While its large cabinet housed vacuum tubes, batteries were installed under the floorboards. A rather cumbersome horn mounted above the windshield served as a loudspeaker.

By the close of the thirties, a range of models featuring remote control tuning were introduced. Soon, decorative speaker grills emulated the grandiose chrome of the jukebox. Overly embellished with thick, gleaming chrome, the parallel ribs of the automotive speaker compartment comprised a substantial part of the dash. The car radio had arrived—in style!

As automatic transmissions came into use, improved radios that tuned themselves followed, mimicking the ease of their powertrain cousins. Zenith debuted its "Radionic" unit, featuring foot control, in 1946. One year later, Delco chose to continue the trend with its steering-column-controlled "Signal Seeking" model. Consumers liked the improvements—and within a few years, over 7 million motorists were snapping their fingers to the sounds.

It wasn't long before young listeners availed themselves of the convenience and discovered a new reason to borrow the family car: music! By the time most amplifying tubes and components were miniaturized in 1951, WJW disc jockey Allen "Moon Dog" Freed began spinning a new type of music in Cleveland. As the phenomenon spread, push-button tuners with improved circuitry were just the thing to capture the new sounds of "rock'n'roll."

Suddenly, dashboards came alive with an electrified beat, galvanizing a new generation of drive-in car customers together with its hypnotic rhythms. While carhops stepped in time to the thumping backbeat of the bass, listeners were mesmerized by the raucous sounds.

Future teenage idols sang of drag racing, dancing, and romance, one of the radical new Fender electric guitars twanging out the battle cry for changes to come. From chromed slits in the dashboard, the music of a new generation made its way into the hearts and minds of youthful car culture.

Now inseparable, the drive-in eatery, the automobile, and the car radio became one. The act of parking under the muted circle of drive-in neon with your date—a cheeseburger in one hand, the other around your girl—was now a complete ritual. For couples huddled together at drive-ins all across America, the warm glow emanating from the tuning dial became a new communal campfire.

More than just a novelty, the car radio was now an electronic bridge to a new era. A point of connection between the vanguards waiting for their moment to come—one with time for new ideas, new morals, and new music. "One, two, three o'clock, four o'clock rock ...." ∎

5144-27

Wolfman Jack Doing His Stuff
The howling, prowling Wolfman Jack was the behind-the-scenes alter-ego for the teenagers in the movie American Graffiti *of 1973. Without him, rock'n'roll* would not have been the same. Frozen Popsicle anyone? Museum of Modern Art/Film Stills Archive, Copyright © by Universal City Studios, Inc. Courtesy of MCA Publishing Rights, a Division of MCA Inc.

continued from page 137

profit margins, and fewer hassles with employees brought the drive-in industry to the edge.

While tiny transistors replaced vacuum tubes, America's perceptions about everyday life were changing. Postwar prosperity became equated with faster cars, faster shopping, faster working, faster living, faster eating, and finally, faster dying. Flickering images flashing on the television screen became a substitute for real life, re-formatting the way people thought about authority, automobiles, and the food they consumed while cruising through the roadside carnival.

As society began its self-inflicted launch towards a higher speed, new ideas and dreams and frustrations were slowly taking root in the youth of the nation. In the new environment of automation, respect for the establishment was eroding as social misfits known as juvenile delinquents, or JDs, made their presence known. Trouble was just around the corner for the outdoor car eatery in the form of rowdy behavior, vandalism, and endless loitering. As heat lamps were switched on in franchised fast-food kitchens all across America, the infrared glow above the stack of pre-made hamburgers was a signal that the nation's drive-in restaurants would never be the same. The heyday was about to end. ■

Dari-ette Drive-In Speaker Box
During the 1950s, manufacturers developed a variety of drive-in communications gear. The hand-held speaker box and microphone combination was one of the most widely used designs, taking the nation's drive-in customers into the electronic age. This pole-mounted speaker box continues to offer radio-relayed orders to the kitchen at the Dari-ette Drive-In in St. Paul, Minnesota. Michael Dregni

Dari-ette Drive-In
Left, the Dari-ette on St. Paul, Minnesota's, east side began life as a simple ice cream stand in the 1950s, adding on drive-in parking, speaker boxes, and a small inside dining area in later years—all built around that original building. Dari-ette is famous for its Italian spaghetti sauce, and is probably the only drive-in ever to offer spaghetti as a side dish with a hamburger. The rich, spicy sauce is also available for take out by the pint, quart, or gallon. Michael Dregni

Hicks Drive-In Restaurant
Hick's Kentucky drive-in specialized in steaks, chops, and chicken dinners. At one time, it was a major food stop for motorists making their way down the Dixie Highway. Caufield and Shook Collection, Photographic Archives, University of Louisville

Hicks Drive-In Interior
Right, the interior of Hick's Drive-In featured many of the futuristic building materials of the 1940s and 1950s. Glass block comprised the dining counter. Caufield and Shook Collection, Photographic Archives, University of Louisville

A HEAVEN FOR HOT RODS

During the time of postwar prosperity, America's love affair with the motorcar turned to obsession. Automotive manufacturers turned out a parade of new models and soon, the desire for bigger, flashier, more comfortable vehicles turned to nationwide lust. Unofficially, the timeworn styles were dead: rocketlike tailfins, massive grills, acres of chrome, and a cushioned ride were in.

For Detroit's auto companies, 1955 proved to be a banner year; all records were exceeded as production reached 9 million vehicles! As the consumer frenzy for new models reached its peak, a surplus of outmoded flivvers were soon retired. Former favorites were sold as used cars to new owners or eventually handed down to children coming of age. Those

exceeding their limit of usefulness were unceremoniously dumped.

In road-dense cities such as Los Angeles, New York, and Detroit—where cars and culture mixed—suburban neighborhoods were often littered with discarded vehicles. Backyards, driveways, and vacant lots became the final resting grounds for many abandoned jalopies. Parked among weeds, they were left to rust—or to wait for their day of revitalization.

Fortunately, their time away from the fast-track was limited. A steady supply of teenagers reaching the age of eligibility for a driver's license took immediate advantage of the surplus. Eager to join the fast lane of motoring in the most economical way possible, a majority of unused car parts and bodies were efficiently recycled by enthusiastic teens.

Promptly, Ford flathead engines were removed, transmission casings cannibalized, steering wheels pulled, fenders appropriated, radiators revived, and tires unbolted. During the afterhours sessions at the corner gas station that followed, an unrelated conglomeration of auto parts were carefully united. With a tentative spark of loose ignition wires, a new form of motorized folk art rumbled to life: the American "hot rod."

With a little imagination and a lot of sweat, the burned-out shells of Fords and Chevrolets were transformed into perky T-bucket roadsters, hi-boys, low-boys, lead sleds, and customs. Family sedans junked during the days of the Depression were chopped and channeled, Frenched and flamed, until they bore no resemblance to their original identity. Fenders were removed and bumpers replaced by nerf bars. Even hubcaps became reflective bowls of chrome.

While painted flames became the street rod's ultimate trademark, gray primer assumed dominance as the every man's paint. In the unfinished reality of homemade car construction, perfection was not that important. Missing a few dashboard knobs or door panels didn't make a hot rod any less cool. Searching for elusive parts, working with friends, and taking a show-off cruise thru the local drive-in restaurant was really the most. Unfortunately, the flamboyant displays of speed and the accidents that followed cast a negative light on the hot rod. Ever vigilant for traffic safety and excessive noise, the cops made a living out of harassing the homebuilt carboys—even when they reserved their high-speed sprints for the quarter-mile strip. For the establishment, the hot rodder and juvenile delinquent became one.

Sure, there were a lot of incidents where souped-up vehicles screamed out of the drive-in with trays still attached—milkshake glasses and silverware trailing behind in a cloud of dust. So what? It was only a small part of growing up, a brief moment in the timeline of the road when the drive-in restaurant really was the heaven for hot rods. ∎

Cruise Night
A deuce coupe (1932 Ford) with a chopped top sits proudly at a California Bob's Big Boy —once a popular haven for hot rods in Southern California. ©1994 Kent Bash

RUTH FORKE, TEXAS PIG STAND

Ruth Forke began her job as a carhop when she was only sixteen years old. It all started back in 1939 when a downstairs neighbor was working as a curb server at the Flores Street Pig Stand in San Antonio. Dressed in a fetching ensemble consisting of a blue jacket with four pockets, gray slacks adorned with a dark blue stripe, and a gray "air cadet" hat trimmed in blue, she was a sight that conjured up all the images of patriotism and service at a time when many young boys were going off to war.

When the neighbor left for work, Ruth caught sight of her snappy uniform, shifting her own imagination into overdrive. Suddenly, Ruth wanted to be a carhop too. A short while later, Ruth joined the Pig Stand ranks. She commuted to work on the bus and frequently fielded questions from passengers curious about her uniform (everyone thought she was an Air Force girl). For a teenager, this public notoriety was a lot of fun. Eventually, the military-style uniforms were replaced by more feminine styles, including a motif comprised of a satin dress and white boots.

Fortunately, there was more to the Pig Stands than just fancy uniforms: Working a double-shift, Ruth could often pull in $80–$90 in one night! While the wages of 10¢ per hour were minimal pay, the tips were phenomenal. Of course, it was a lot of hard work—labor that eventually paid off in a management position. Ultimately, illness cut Ruth's career short in the mid-eighties, forcing her to leave the drive-in business for good. "If I could, I would still be working there today," she says. Working as a Pig Stands carhop was very, very good for Ruth Forke. ∎

DOUMAR'S CONES AND BARBECUE

*"Amidst the growing atmosphere of fast food banality,
Al Doumar rediscovered his hook—a bonafide skill and culinary folk talent
that none of the modern burger shacks could ever hope to replicate."*

Today, Norfolk, Virgina's, Monticello Avenue is paved over with a dizzying procession of fast-food restaurants. Illuminated marquees vie for the attention of passing traffic, obscuring the view of the roadside. In an unceasing battle for the motorist's dollar, franchised giants wage an unending war. Burger King, McDonald's, Kentucky Fried Chicken, Hardee's, and Wendy's all fight for dominance with meal deals and price combo strategies.

Right there, smack dab in the middle of it all, Albert Doumar sells North Carolina-style barbecue (made with vinegar) and ice cream cones, content to take on all the competition. He's been holding his own for the past sixty years now, ever since his father George's ice cream concession at Virginia's Ocean View Park was obliterated by the hurricane in 1933. Back then, his dad had exclusive rights to sell frozen desserts at the seaside resort. When the winds of change literally destroyed his operation, all that remained were the machinery and fixtures used to make his living.

Albert Doumar and Doumar's Drive-In
Albert Doumar's Virginia drive-in is straddled by two of today's largest fast-food chains: Wendy's and Taco Bell. In fact, almost the entire stretch of Norfolk's Monticello Avenue is paved over with fast-food outlets! Hardees, Burger King, and a trio of McDonald's restaurants dominate the strip. To make matters worse, another fast-food chain is planning to build a structure right across the street. Does all the competition worry Doumar? Not in the least! He is a true survivor in the competitive arena of drive-in food. © 1994, W. S. McIntosh

Among the debris sat what would one day become the saving grace of a new enterprise: a small, four-iron waffle machine made of cast iron and brass. To the unknowing, it may have appeared to be another piece of junk to be cleared away, but to Doumar it was much more. This was, after all, the very machine inspired by the waffle iron Uncle Abe used to create the World's Fair Cornucopia in 1904. With it came the power to produce the best cones ever tasted by man! The only requirements to reap a bounty of 200 cones an hour were hand-eye coordination and a knack for old-fashioned showmanship.

In short order, the small machine joined the rest of the salvageable equipment and was moved farther inland to Norfolk's Monticello Avenue. The family operation reopened in 1934 as a drive-in restaurant with carhop service and offered barbecue pork sandwiches, limeades, and soda fountain treats to the local patrons. As curb-serving competitors such as Bill's, Frank's, and Bobby's catered to beer-drinking clientele, Doumar's favored the family crowd by featuring delicious waffle cones filled with frosty chocolate, vanilla, strawberry, and butter pecan ice cream.

At the time, the legendary waffle maker that set the Doumar legacy into motion was put into retirement. A much larger, electrically operated unit boasting eighteen irons and forced gas circulation was used to crank out the tasty ice cream holders. Eventually, the cone-spewing behemoth disintegrated and a succession of smaller machines were recruited to manufacture the latticed forms. Meanwhile, the art and style of cone-making passed down so many years ago—Al learned how to make his first cone when he was fourteen—was beginning to be taken for granted.

As franchise after franchise began to set up shop along the boulevard, the climate of competition began to change. Suddenly, all of the barbecue stands began dying out, leaving Doumar's as the last remaining outlet. When the golden arches materialized in 1958, the interest in pork sandwiches faded and business experienced a drop. As the purveyors of convenience foods became absorbed with the flashy promise of a quick hamburger, Al Doumar realized that something had to be done—fast!

Promptly, the "old number one" waffle gizmo was taken out of mothballs and set up on the sidewalk in front of the drive-in. Doumar began pouring batter, flipping irons, and forming cones as he fielded questions from curious customers. The gimmick worked, and soon both young and old were taken in by the unpretentious show. With no artificial flavors, colorings, or preservatives added, mouth-watering cones rolled easily off the seasoned waffle iron (Al calls it "Grandma's Teflon") into the hands of a pleased audience.

Amidst the growing atmosphere of fast food banality, Al Doumar rediscovered his hook—a bonafide skill and culinary folk talent that none of the modern burger shacks could ever hope to replicate. With that talent intact, Doumar's Cones and Barbecue is poised to enter the next century—confident to base a drive-in business on one simple metal machine. ∎

Doumar's Other Drive-In
The enterprising Doumar family expanded operations into Detroit and the Florida area. These drive-ins unfortunately did not survive when the fast-food giants moved into their territory. Preziosi Postcards

Wanda Morris Holding Two Trays
Left, carhop Wanda Morris has worked at Albert Doumar's Norfolk drive-in for over twenty years. She's proven that a carhop can beat an electronic ordering menu and drive-thru window any day of the week. For her, toting two trays filled with the tasty barbecue and ice cream cones that made Doumar's a local legend has become second-nature. © 1994, John Witt, Richmond Newspapers, Inc.

CHAPTER FOUR

DRIVE-IN DEMISE AND RE-RISE

During the twilight of the fifties, youngsters coming of age in America desperately desired a place they could call their own— an up-to-date hangout where they could act freely, make their own choices, listen to their kind of music, and gather with others of like mind. Increasingly disillusioned with the lifestyles of their elders, teenagers began to break free from societal constraints to seek a measure of personal autonomy.

Social pressures peaked when planned communities modeled after Levittown transformed farmland into middle-class conformity. To make the dream of a home with white picket fence affordable for returning veterans, room designs were small—only large enough for studying and sleeping. As a result, entertaining friends was difficult. Besides, adults screened visitors and dictated dinner time. As mother toiled over her new electric range defrosting peas for supper, father switched on "The Texaco Star Theater" and reclined in his easy chair with paper and pipe. The same scenario was repeated in row after row of identical homes on carbon-copy streets. While this model of postwar life was ideal for adults, it was not so idyllic for teenagers.

Fortunately, there was one outlet where the young citizens of suburbia could exercise their freedom. At any time, day or night, one could escape the stifling confines of the tract-house lifestyle and find fulfillment with a sack of hot French fries and a cheeseburger. The only requirements: the ownership of a car or the ability to borrow one. Within minutes, one could motor down to the local milkshake watering hole and enter a new world: slap the car into park, kill the engine, order some food, flirt with the carhops, smoke some cigarettes, fiddle with the radio, or cuddle with a sweetheart...free from parental control. For the teen, the drive-in restaurant became a home away from home.

Congregating at the local tray food retreat soon became an obsession of the adolescent.

Steak 'n Shake Kids and Shakes
Right, hunger, a station wagon full of kids, and a busy mom meant only one thing during the 1960s: a trip to Steak 'n Shake! With window trays stacked to the hilt with Tru-Flavor milkshakes and all sorts of food delights, it was a time a child would remember for the rest of his life. Courtesy Steak 'n Shake, Inc.

Sonic Drive-In
Previous pages, cruising down to the local drive-in restaurant was a popular pastime of youth during the 1950s and 1960s. On almost any night of the week, teenagers could be found there in great numbers— socializing, eating hamburgers, and tinkering with their cars. Back then, spying a shiny 1955 Chevrolet (Clare Patterson, owner) or a classic 1939 Cadillac (Dan Daniels, owner) would not have been at all unusual. East Central, Wichita, Kansas.

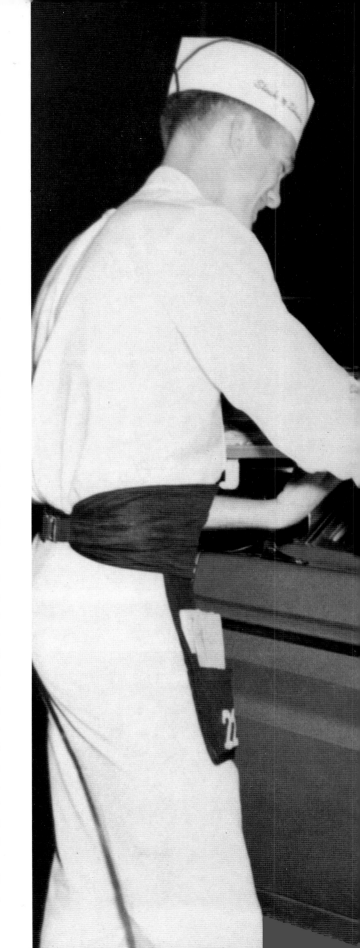

Along with pep rallies, football games, and the high school hop, this open-air gathering place run on liquid cola and ground beef was an appropriate venue for teenage socialization. After the final school bell, it became a popular destination to rendezvous with peers, find romantic interests, and come fender to fender with rivals. Without the constant scrutiny found at indoor eateries, kids could relax. Best of all, one wasn't required to leave the security of the car. If desired, the entire visit to the drive-in could be experienced from the comfort of the automotive shell. Automotive prowess now defined one's social status.

As America entered the sixties, the teenage takeover of the nation's drive-ins began to degrade the atmosphere for others. Now, the family trade was avoiding the carhop domain entirely—and who could blame them? In the most extreme situations, cars remained parked for long periods as boisterous teenagers blasted loud rock'n'roll music on their car radios. Amidst the din of yelling and all manner of carrying on, many kids drank beer and engaged in fist fights. When guitarist Chuck Berry released "No Particular Place to Go" in 1964, it sounded like he had the drive-ins in mind. Finally, the nation's restless rabble of teenagers had an anthem for their nightly ritual of "cruisin' and playin' the radio."

By 1966, over 78 million cars packed America's corridors of asphalt, making the inner circle at the drive-in eatery a crowded place. With nothing to do and no place to do it, food businesses along the strip became waypoints for gasoline-guzzling adolescents.

Rowdyism replaced relaxation. To park and enjoy a meal became almost impossible, as cars stalled for hours in the lots, their occupants "hanging out" until something eventful happened—while food and drink orders were kept to a minimum. Cars never left and paying customers were hindered from using the drive-ins at all. Revenues began to suffer.

Ironically, the drive-ins themselves were partly to blame: with circular layouts providing ease of access and traffic flow, they invited habitual cruising. As a result, a continuous train

CRUISIN' THE MAIN STREET STRIP

During the 1950s, it seemed that all of America's commerce had suddenly become an extension of the automobile. Society mobilized, taking entertainment at drive-in theaters and eating meals from behind the

Lovers At Doumar's Drive-In
Gloria Harper of Oscar Smith High School and Tommy Bland, all-state full-back of Maury High School, dine at Doumar's Drive-In in 1956. This favorite high school hangout was paid full tribute in the 1956 Oscar Smith High School Year-book. The fifties—we remember them well: the boy, the girl, the car, and of course, the drive-in! Courtesy of Albert Doumar

dashboard. Shopping centers, gas stations, supermarkets, car dealerships, and drive-in food stands became the new crossroads for social connection.

So dominant was the influence of the motorcar that even ordinary routes of passage became part of the action. Without any stimulating activities to call their own, the commercial "strip" became the playground for adolescent youth. Hypnotized by the prosperous imagery and inebriated with the freedom of the automobile, teens clogged the major business corridors more than ever before.

For the postwar generation weaned on personal mobility, the act of "cruising" quickly became a national pastime. Since gasoline was cheap and egress over the public roads free, recreational driving reached a new level of popularity. "Motorvating" down bustling Main Street to see the sights, meet members of the opposite sex, and show off one's car was elevated to a defined social activity. The horseless carriage had evolved into a portable amusement compartment.

In towns small and large, Saturday nights were reluctantly relinquished for the motorized rituals of youth. As the sun gave way to the electric hum of neon, the asphalt stage came alive with the sounds of tuned headers and dashboard radios. One carload at a time, the main "drag" welcomed four-wheel contestants onto the playing field. By 10 o'clock, the divided blacktop was packed from curb to curb with music and motion.

As the aroma of cheeseburgers punctuated each block, all manner of motor vehicle took to the streets to see and be seen. Donning ducktail doos, "low riders" moved along pavement in white-walled lead sleds. Garage mechanics who knew how to mate three deuces with a flathead rode herd in custom hot rods. Jocks and the so-called social elite joined the frenzy, piloting classy Corvettes and other stock vehicles. For the unfortunate few without wheels, the family station wagon proved a dismal contender.

Regardless of the vehicle type used, the basic parameters of cruising quickly crystallized: guide a car down the strip at slow speed, wave at friends, and attempt to make new ones. For the boys, looking cool was a high priority. Racking the pipes and laying a little rubber at the green became part of the show. Amused by the boulevard strut of the motorized male, carloads of girls engaged in "Chinese fire drills" and preened to capture their share of the attention.

If the action reached a level of boredom for either group, any number of local eateries could be frequented for a change of atmosphere. To avoid spending a lot of money and being kicked out, only one of the car occupants would order French fries and Coke. At each drive-in to follow, the restrained ordering procedure was repeated, until ultimately all passengers had eaten. For a minimal expenditure, a carload of teenagers could cruise the town and do "the loop."

By the end of the fifties, the car-crazed high school crowd had established important tenets of motorized culture. Riding the Main continued to root itself as an established tradition of American youth. Van Nuys Boulevard, Sunset Strip, or the countless other roads across the nation—it didn't matter. A full tank of gas, a warm evening, and a carload of friends would always mean one thing: cruising the Main Street strip. ∎

of unwanted automobiles streamed unhindered from the main road. Kids rolled their tires at an excruciatingly slow clip—scanning the stalls for boyfriends, girlfriends, and acquaintances. When they reached the end of the lot and exited to the street, a loop of the block was made and the circuit repeated until the night ended or they were chased down by a police cruiser. Locked in by the heavy traffic, those already positioned in the service lanes remained there. Congestion, confusion, and arguments resulted.

Although only one-fourth of the nation's drive-ins reported problems with youthful customers, the situation appeared out of control to many. With over 2,000 drive-in eateries, California experienced the brunt of the problems, followed by Texas and the Great Lakes regions. Isolated incidents cast a bad light on them all, including those that employed techniques to control exuberant customers.

During the mid-1960s, the establishment's negative view of the drive-in was exacerbated

AN AMERICAN INTERNATIONAL PICTURE

by a chilling report from Camarillo, California. From the first day he purchased The Bullet Drive-In, owner Violney Robison could tell he was going to have problems with his business.

continued on page 158

Hot-Rod Girl *and* **Hot Rod Gang**
Hot rods powered a new breed of youngsters to cruise Main Street and hang out at the drive-ins. Called juvenile delinquents, or JDs, they were personified by James Dean in Rebel Without A Cause, as well as the slew of B-budget exploitation films that ran in a never-ending chase across the screens of America's drive-in theaters. Ron Main/Main Attractions

Second Life for a Drive-In
Left, Minneapolis' two Nora's restaurants were once hopping Porky's Drive-Ins located at both ends of the Lake Street strip like magnetic poles for hot-rod cruisers. Both Porky's turned off their neon in the 1970s. In the 1980s, the car stalls were walled in and the drive-ins reopened as indoor sitdown restaurants.

DINING AT THE DRIVE-IN THEATER

MOTION PICTURES UNDER THE STARS... ROMANCE BY MOONLIGHT

The **DRIVE-IN**

SOME INTERESTING FACTS AND INFORMATION ABOUT THE WORLD'S LARGEST AND MOST BEAUTIFUL DRIVE-IN THEATRE

AT WAUKEGAN AND GOLF ROADS...JUST WEST OF EVANSTON

Drive-In Theater Brochure
As the brochure promised, "Romance by Moonlight." Courtesy Chuck Sturm

In the early thirties, Richard Hollingshead had a grand idea. Why not show moving pictures in the great outdoors where people could watch from their cars? After all, the drive-in restaurant was a popular gathering spot. Extending this in-your-car convenience to include the silver screen seemed only natural.

Tentatively, he proceeded to position a projector on the hood of his car. Nailed to a nearby tree, a makeshift screen became the beam's focus. Hollingshead like what he saw, and three years later, the basic elements of his outdoor theater concept were refined and patented. In June of 1933, the first outdoor theater in America where "people could enjoy talkies in their car" opened for business in Camden, New Jersey.

As the novelty of viewing moving pictures within a motorcar slowly gained popularity, car customers realized something was missing: they were hungry! Claudette Colbert's hitchhiking scene in *It Happened One Night* was no time to drive off to the neighborhood Pig Stand. Fortunately, operators were already one frame ahead. "Dining room" was already being added to the varied list of convenient automotive attributes.

By the late forties, most food concessions at the "Ozoners" were basic stands. Positioned at one or two serving stations, counter girls took the orders, made food, and returned change. Inefficient and slow, it was a frustrating process for those anxious to return to their vehicles. During intermission, conditions only worsened. A throng of customers converged on the ill-equipped shacks, turning off eager film fans in the process.

Further investigation revealed much of the snack bar patronage was lost by people not wanting to leave their cars. Often, a long walk to the stand was necessary. Carrying food by hand proved limiting since only a finite amount of burgers and beverages could be hand-held.

Bringing food out to the customers was a much better method. By the mid-1940s, vendors toting shoulder-carried snack-packs loudly hawked their wares among the sea of rubber and chrome. At many theaters, tricycles were introduced to cover long distances. These were soon superseded by elaborate pushcarts capable of holding all sorts of food. Summoned by cards placed on the windshield, these "Buffeterias" roamed the lot in search of hungry customers.

Still, there were problems: as the diminutive casters of these mobile vending carts forged a path through the gravel, patrons nearby would be disturbed by the noise. The shear weight of the 100-pound supply of hot dogs, soft drinks, and popcorn made them difficult to maneuver. Artificial viewing burms in the viewing lot did not help matters.

At the dawn of the fifties, a solution arrived in the form of the "talk-back system." Hungry movie watchers at the Park Drive-In in Greensboro, North Carolina, could now depress a button on the side of their speaker, instantly summoning a central switchboard operator. Carhops would pick up the orders and deliver, while pleased car customers eased back into the vinyl and enjoyed the film, without missing a single scene.

Eventually, the impracticality of in-car service lost out at the rampatoriums. Dimly illuminated lots were dangerous, a tangle of speaker cords and trash a detriment. The centrally located snack-bar, or "profiteria," became the safest choice. No longer commercially viable, carhops were out; cafeteria-style was in. Drive-in movie dining entered headlong into the netherworld of self-serve. ∎

Drive-In THEATRE
REFRESHMENTS

Delightful and Tasty Refreshments served in Your Car while You enjoy the Picture

IF YOU DESIRE REFRESHMENTS DURING THE SHOW PLACE THIS CARD UNDER YOUR WINDSHIELD WIPER
UNIFORMED ATTENDANT WILL SERVE YOU

PRICE LIST

How Many?

Coca-Cola (Ice cold in bottles) .10c
ALL OTHER SOFT DRINKS.....
HAMBURGERS—Jumbo Si...
RED HOTS .....
MALTED MILKS—
MILK SHAKES ..
BLACK COWS ...
ICE CREAM CUPS.
CHOCOLATE ICE C
COFFEE (with pure
FRESH HOT POPCOR
SALTED PEANUTS ..
POTATO CHIPS ......
CIGARETTES ....

RESTAURANT IS LOCATED IN THE CENTER OF AISLE 5

"Another Drive-In Service"

FREE! FREE! FREE!
ADMITS
CAR and DRIVER
Golden Spike DRIVE-IN THEATRE
114th and Dodge Sts.— TE. 2211
Courtesy of .....
GOOD ANY DAY EXCEPT Saturday, Sunday, Holidays

---

*W*hy not show moving pictures in the great outdoors where people could watch from their cars? After all, the drive-in restaurant was a popular gathering spot. In June of 1933, the first outdoor theater in America where "people could enjoy talkies in their car" opened for business in Camden, New Jersey.

Drive-In Theater Card
For service, you simply placed the card underneath your windshield wiper and the uniformed attendant was at your beck and call. Courtesy Chuck Sturm

Abandoned Drive-In
Today, most of the drive-in restaurants adored during the fifties have disappeared from the roadside landscape, such as this relic in Fort Worth, Texas. While car service relics are hard to come by, some decaying survivors can be found in regions where the real estate prices have not exceeded common sense.

continued from page 155
Right away, youths drove in after school and began to plug up his driveways. They double-parked all over the lot and refused to move their vehicles when asked nicely. What's worse, they ignored the rules of deportment, substituting disrespect and anarchy.

When Robison went out to the lot one night to ask the kids to leave, bedlam broke out as they shouted him down and refused to budge. He returned to the store room to gain his composure and fell to a heart attack. Meanwhile, the delinquents in the parking lot

were carrying on and laughing about how they had won out. Robison's unfortunate death pointed to a system that needed rethinking given the type of "patrons" now ruining it for the majority.

When neighborhoods adjacent to America's drive-ins began complaining to local government about the mayhem, municipal ordinances were introduced to curb the unrestrained curb servers. Laws outlawed the act of cruising around in an automobile simply "for the thrill of it" and even banned loitering in parking lots. Curfews cut back afterhours traffic. Some regulations dictated that litter be cleared regularly, while others called for fences to enclose the ruckus. When shielding the public from the commotion proved ineffective, a handful of ordinances attempted to eliminate carhop service completely. As if they didn't have enough problems, drive-in owners were being held legally accountable for what happened on, and even near, their lots.

For many establishments, the ordinances alone were not enough to stem the growing tide of teenagers. Many went on to contract the services of police officers and posted patrols to preclude fights and other rambunctious behavior. Entry gates were also installed. As silent sentinels, they effectively controlled exit by way of a token or quarter. If a customer drove in and ordered food, a free exit coin was given. When a teen attempted to slink through with the express purpose of checking out the scene, he was required to pay for the liberty. Unfortunately, this controlling attempt

Coffee-Shop Sign of the Times
California led the nation with coffee-shops during the sixties, popularizing the idea that interior seating served more customers with less hassle. It didn't take long for the notion to spread nationwide, decimating the drive-ins. Broadway Pig Stand, San Antonio, Texas

Decayed Drive-In Sign Pointing Back in Time
Left, another sign of the times.... By the end of the 1960s, many of the classic drive-ins were boarded up and ready for the bulldozer. This old drive-in sign along the Berlin Turnpike in Connecticut is a streetside survivor.

Classic Sign
Right, Speedy points the way to the Downey, California, McDonald's. David Fetherston

Classic McDonald's
Below, one of the last of the early McDonald's still standing, this classic restaurant in Downey, California, was slated for demolition in 1994. David Fetherston

to curtail the craving for cruising only aggravated the situation. It annoyed the responsible customers, eliminating two reasons why the drive-ins became so popular in the first place: convenience and easy access.

The government put in their two cents worth during the White House Conference on Natural Beauty in 1965. Spearheaded by civic activist Ladybird Johnson, legislation was proposed to eliminate "endless corridors walled in by neon, junk, and ruined landscape." The meeting culminated in two bills that complicated the drive-in owner's job. Suddenly, businesses that served motorists were responsible for upgrading the nation's roadscape! Junkyards, gas stations, hot dog stands, billboards, and finally, drive-in restaurants were put on the list as potential "eyesores." Once a loud

continued on page 166

STEAK 'N SHAKE TAKHOMASAK

*"Belt's first 'Steak 'n Shake Drive-In opened in
Normal, Illinois, and proved anything but. Unlike other curb-stands,
his outfit catered to the individual mood of customers."*

While California restauranteurs were restyling the drive-in as circular monument, A. H. "Gus" Belt was working on something more important: improving the hamburger. In 1934, his efforts culminated in the "Steakburger," a seared sandwich of ground beef fortified by fine cuts of T-bone, strip, and sirloin. When he teamed it with a hand-dipped shake, it became an irresistible meal.

Belt's first "Steak 'n Shake" Drive-In opened in Normal, Illinois, and proved anything but. Unlike other curb-stands, his outfit catered to the individual mood of customers. If someone wanted to dine within their car, that was fine. When inclement weather called for dinner inside, it was available. Patrons with itchy feet were accommodated, too: sacks could be packed to go or meals eaten at a counter.

It didn't take long for this innovative "four-way service" to seize the interest of those who liked to dine-in-a-hurry. By 1948, the first drive-in had grown into many and motorfood fans in St. Louis were introduced to the versatility of "Takhomasak." Indiana was next, the tasty reputation of the mouth-watering steakburger spreading throughout the state.

Numerous outposts followed with white-tiled buildings edged in black. On their rooftops, painted signboards featured the words "Steak 'n Shake" in bold lettering. Out along the overhang, smaller signs reminded the hungry of the "Genuine Chili" and "Tru-Flavor" shakes, teasing tastebuds with aplomb.

Best of all, every part of the cooking process was visible to customers. Spotless kitchens draped in stainless steel were designed in such a manner so that those in the dining room could see grill men frying and shake men mixing. Strategically placed windows allowed customers parked in their cars to view the preparations. For the patron tired of inferior quality, it was a confidence builder. "In Sight, It Must Be Right" became a popular slogan.

Unfortunately, Steak 'n Shake founder Gus Belt died in 1954. But by then, his admirable program to improve the flavor of the hamburger was firmly established. Today, that legacy is continued as modern Steak 'n Shake eateries continue the tradition. Although carhop service is no longer offered, current owner Consolidated Products, Inc., has managed to inject a measure of fifties ambiance into its new structures. Nostalgic components are used throughout: glass brick adorns entry vestibules and nostalgic awnings decorate the facades. On each corner, rounded "wings" adorned in neon anchor the design to the roadway, rekindling the era of Art Moderne.

Inside, the flavor-packed steakburgers formulated by Gus Belt sixty years ago are still made the same way. At over 135 modern Steak 'n Shake outlets located throughout Missouri, Indiana, Illinois, Georgia, Florida, Ohio, Kentucky, Iowa, and Kansas, food is served using real glassware and china. Every entree is prepared to customer order and pre-cooking abhorred.

With burger boredom now an unfortunate byproduct of motoring's modern age, it's encouraging to see that certain recipes remain cherished. After all, the American hamburger is just a hamburger. The Steak 'n Shake steakburger is much more. "It's a Meal!" ■

Steak 'n Shake Drive-In
Built on the concept of a Steakburger and hand-dipped milkshake, Steak 'n Shake is one of America's original drive-in restaurants. This drive-in is located on old Route 66, on the outskirts of St. Louis, Missouri. ©1994 Craig Curtin

Steak 'n Shake Balloons and Beetle
Balloons for the kids (and adults) were an effective way to excite customers and develop loyal clientele. For Steak 'n Shake, it was a visible way to attract attention when opening new outlets. Still, the food garnered the most attention; the delicious Steakburger was often reward enough for the hungry motorist. Courtesy Steak 'n Shake, Inc.

Steak 'n Shake
Left, by the 1960s, the Steak 'n Shake chain of drive-in restaurants was well known throughout the Midwest. Gus Belt's original formula for serving up a complete meal of Steakburger and hand-dipped milkshake became a roadside standard. "It's a Meal" was the company's popular slogan. Because the customer could see the order being prepared, "In Sight It Must Be Right" joined it as car-dining catch-phrase. Courtesy Steak 'n Shake, Inc.

Steak 'n Shake Carhops
By the 1950s, drive-in restaurants had developed quite a list of do's and don'ts. Standing erect while taking the order without resting the checkbook on the car was standard procedure. At Steak 'n Shake Drive-Ins throughout the Midwest, carhops adopted the styles pioneered by the early service station attendant: black bow-tie, slacks, and white shirt. Courtesy Steak 'n Shake, Inc.

FROM FISH BRINE TO KETCHUP

Ahhh…that tangy, thick, and sticky condiment known as ketchup. Where would American roadfood be without it? Certainly, drive-ins, diners, coffee-shops, and in many cases, fine restaurants, wouldn't be the same. Burgers would be bland, fries embarrassed by nakedness, and hot dogs robbed of their bite. In a world devoid of the red sauce, Archie Bunker would have starved.

Historians trace the ancestry of the zesty mixture as far back as the Roman Empire. Ancient cooks created a sauce from the entrails of dried fish they called "garum," a highly prized addition to the dinner table. The more familiar word "ketchup" however, probably had its origins in the 1690s, from what the Chinese called "kôechiap" or "kê-tsiap." Created from the brine of pickled fish or shellfish, it was the Orient's answer to a flavor-enhancing food additive.

After the East India Company opened trade with the Far East during the sixteenth century, the port markets of Singapore became a favorite place for sailors. There, exotic dishes accompanied by a tasty hot sauce dubbed "kechap" were hyped by Malaysian vendors. The dressing became an immediate favorite and promptly exported when the seafarers returned home (the Dutch renamed it Ketjap). Before too long, frazzled housewives began experimenting with the recipe, attempting to recreate the tantalizing concoction their well-traveled mates were raving about.

It came as no surprise that *Mrs. Harrison's Housekeeper's Pocketbook* and *Mrs. Glasse's Cookery Book* began featuring recipes during the 1700s to aid the creative cook in her adventures. But since the exotic ingredients used in the Indonesian mixture were not available in England, a variety of other staples were cleverly substituted. Ketchups made of mushrooms became the first choice, followed by purees based on tomatoes, walnuts, anchovies, and even oysters.

Despite the variety, the idea of ketchup as a food enhancer began to grow in popularity. Sailors returning to America eventually brought the sauce across the Atlantic, adding tomatoes gathered during expeditions to Mexico or the West Indies to the sauce. Their families loved it, and soon tomato seeds were planted so that they might have a ready supply of the prime ingredient.

Now, women had to add the task of mixing up large batches of condiment to their wifely duties. It was a laborious job, requiring an entire day of stirring just to ensure that the pulp didn't stick to the bottom of the pot. Henry J. Heinz saw his opportunity in this work and wasted no time adding ketchup to the line of condiments he was producing for sale. In 1876, he began to manufacture and bottle America's first commercially processed tomato ketchup.

Since then, ketchup has risen to its place of prominence as the supreme condiment for the masses. The distinctive multi-faceted bottle has established itself as an icon of the fast food table-top, taking its rightful place along with salt and pepper shakers and rectangular napkin dispensers. For the frenzied aficionados who thump, shake, and pour the piquant sauce upon every conceivable foodstuff known to man, there is no other substance like it.

Move over, mayonnaise, mustard, and secret sauce—tomato ketchup reigns unchallenged as the primo junk food compliment from coast to coast. Call it ketchup, catsup, or catchup—nobody really cares. Just be sure there is a full bottle on the table, an ample supply in the squeeze pump, and at least a half dozen of those little plastic packets in the bag. ∎

Heinz Ketchup ad, 1925
In today's world of roadside dining, it's becoming difficult to find an actual ketchup bottle or mustard pot residing at the table arrangement of any fast-food restaurant. To properly dress a quick roadside meal with the right quantity required to satisfy, a small fistful of impregnable packets must be carefully opened without splattering their contents. The frivolous days when streams of ketchup flowed freely from bottles have passed. Courtesy Heinz, Inc.

During the twilight of the fifties, youngsters coming of age in America desperately desired a place they could call their own—an up-to-date hangout where they could act freely. Fortunately, there was one outlet. At any time, day or night, one could escape the stifling confines of the tract-house lifestyle and find fulfillment with a sack of hot French fries and cheeseburger.

continued from page 160

attention-getter, America's carhop eatery had no choice but to conform—to be seen but not heard! In fear of litigation and strangulation by red tape, curb operators kowtowed to the whims of lawmakers and scrambled to improve their appearance.

Waco, Texas, gained notoriety for its beautification efforts when Jim Kimbell, vice-president of Kim's Drive-In, implemented a few simple changes in landscaping. "Let's put up a building that belongs to its surroundings…one that improves the neighborhood but doesn't embarrass it. Not a neon palace, but something subtle and attractive that will blend with its neighbors," he proclaimed. Kim's proceeded to do just that, softening their service building and canopy by facing them with cedar shake shingles. The colorful geometric doo-dads that adorned the drive-ins only a few years ago were out of style. Now, shrubs with thorns—strategically placed wherever teenagers might congregate—were all the rage. It was all part of blending into the environment.

Sadly, the carhop could no longer blend with her surroundings either. When compared to counter servers at the fast-food burger stand and the well-coifed waitress at the indoor eatery, she appeared out of place. To make matters worse, the image of the carhop as a wholesome girl was fading. As early as the fifties, the once-eminent carhop was showing some tarnish. The abbreviated skirts and revealing uniforms once regarded as advantageous for business were now blamed for attracting the wrong element. When Big Boy hamburger king Robert Wian ventured forth into the Dallas market to open a new franchise, he experienced trouble recruiting local girls. Was the drive-in theater's tawdry reputation as a "passion pit" rubbing off on its road-food cousin? Probably; Wian had to fly a team of twenty carhops in from California.

While the drive-in industry battled these problems, the value of real estate spiraled up.

In dense cities such as Los Angeles, modest units like Simon's and Herbert's could no longer generate enough revenues to sustain the land they occupied and both operations were defunct by the sixties. The answer was maximum customer turnover, a program perfectly suited to indoor coffee-shops. In 1961, *Drive-In* magazine reported that of the 209 restaurants built over the last ten years, 191 were of the "sit-down" type, the majority being coffee-shops. Though the Midwest was largely unaffected, motor canteens began dominating California, relegating carhop service to an accessory. The trend was understandable, since an indoor format offered more advantages to the modern restauranteur.

In the same *Drive-In* article, Matt Shipman (founder of Ship's coffee-shops) related one of the main reasons for the disappearance of the drive-in format: some people regard eating in their car as uncomfortable. Shipman remembers the time comedian Bob Hope ordered a drink and a sandwich at Tiny Naylor's Drive-In. When the carhop delivered the order, she pinned him behind the wheel with an oversized serving tray. With the food only inches away, Hope politely inquired if he could have a "short fork!"

More seriously, coffee-shops reduced business fluctuation due to the weather. Even in sunny Southern California, an overcast day could cause revenues to vary from $800 to $900. The contrast between a drive-in's summer volume and winter business was often as much as 60 percent. What's more, the average check for each coffee-shop visit was higher. Pleasant surroundings encouraged more food ordering and less rush. As a bridge to the modern age (where casual wear could be worn for all occasions), the coffee-shops were as comfortable for the well-dressed businessman as they were for the sportsman right off the golf course.

On a Los Angeles drive during the fifties, Douglas Haskell, a writer for *House and*

continued on page 174

Mike's Drive-In Table Service
The well-stacked hamburger meal served with a plate of French fries and extra large Coca-Cola has achieved legendary status in the annals of American roadfood. When teamed with a full bottle of ketchup, salt and pepper, stack of napkins, and rock'n'roll music blaring from a tabletop jukebox, it's a combination that can't be beat. Jukebox control units like this model were standard issue at most of America's diners, coffee-shops, family restaurants, truck stops, greasy spoons, and drive-ins during the 1950s. Forget Muzak piped in from a central speaker— nothing compares to punching up your own musical selections while downing a mouthful of fries. This Crosley Select-o-Matic jukebox is a replica of the original units. Jukebox Courtesy Red Horse Museum

WACO'S DR PEPPER DRINK

Down at The Old Corner Drugstore fountain in Waco, Texas, an imaginative medical school graduate named Charles Alderton formulated the "King of Beverages" in the year 1885.

Alderton was highly fascinated with the soda fountain and observed that patrons often had a difficult time choosing which flavoring to add to their carbonated water. He started to experiment, mixing available flavorings in countless combinations. After eliminating a host of formulations, he succeeded in creating a particularly palatable syrup.

Delighted with the tasty results, drugstore owner Wade Morrison foresaw its great profit potential. Further refinements were made in the formula and within a short time, it was offered to local soda-sippers for judicious sampling.

News of the charismatic blend spread fast, and soon more and more customers were asking for it. Alderton's engaging beverage was soon a jewel in The Old Corner Drugstore's crown. Eventually, it became so popular that nearby

Dr Pepper Vintage Logo
Courtesy Dr Pepper Company

drugstore operators inquired about dispensing it. "Shoot me a Waco" became one of the most popular orders at soda counters throughout Central Texas.

To satisfy the demand, Morrison and Alderton teamed up to mix the syrup by themselves until its phenomenal growth rendered the task impossible. As the number of drugstores and soda parlours interested in the syrup grew, they could no longer keep up with the volume.

Luckily, Texas bottler R. S. Lazenby came to the duo's rescue. After some initial experimentation, he confirmed that the "Waco" mixture was a prime candidate for large-scale bottling. To exclusively package the soda drink and capitalize on its success in the marketplace, he formed a new company.

By 1891, The Artesian Manufacturing & Bottling Company had taken what was once just a soda fountain flavor experiment and turned it into a commercially viable product. The familiar Waco nickname was abandoned and an engaging logo designed to enhance recognition of the popular drink. Repackaged for a mass market, the unique beverage became "Dr. Pepper's Phos-Ferrates."

Conflicting stories detailing the original inspiration of the name eventually surfaced, with a host of players throwing their stories into the pot. Unfortunately, the only one with any truth tells of Morrison's early work at Dr. Charles Pepper's pharmacy in Rural Retreat, Virginia. Apparently, he thought well of the good doctor and adopted his "spicy" surname for the beverage.

Further extrapolation of Morrison's younger days enters the realm of fable: supposedly, he fell in love with the Virginia pharmacist's teenage daughter. According to legend, Pepper wasn't thrilled with this and discouraged the romance. Dejected, Morrison said farewell to both and sought his fortune out West. Years later, he decided Alderton's drink should be called Dr. Pepper—as a tribute.

Regardless of the name's mysterious beginnings, the popularity of Dr Pepper continued to spread nationwide. Wherever the public welcomed a new flavor, it flourished. By the time the first drive-in restaurants were capturing the

1891

Dr Pepper 1891 Logo
Courtesy Dr Pepper Company

*D*own at The Old Corner Drugstore fountain in Waco, Texas, an imaginative medical school graduate named Charles Alderton formulated the "King of Beverages" in the year 1885.

Dr. Charles Alderton Portrait
In 1885, Dr. Charles Alderton developed the "King of Beverages." Alderton's engaging drink was soon the jewel in The Old Corner Drugstore's crown. Eventually, it grew so popular that nearby drugstore operators inquired about dispensing it. "Shoot me a Waco" became one of the most popular orders at soda counters throughout Central Texas. By 1891, the familiar nickname was abandoned and the first official bottle of "Dr. Pepper's Phos-Ferrates" was produced. Courtesy of the Dr Pepper Museum, Waco, Texas

fancy of motorists, the sweet-tasting liquid was already a staple drink of roadside stands.

Assuming its rightful place among the emerging roster of carbonated beverages, Dr Pepper has gone on to become one of the soft drink world's distinct flavors. Whether at 10, 2, or 4 o'clock, it's always in demand by thirsty pilots and passengers of America's automobiles. ∎

THE DOCTOR'S FAVORITE CASE
.......HOME TREATMENT FOR FATIGUE

1926

1926

Dr Pepper Logos With Doc
In 1926, Southwestern Advertising designed its first logo for Dr Pepper in the form of this genial, chubby "doc." Dressed in top hat and sporting a monocle, he was to convey the very essence of the soft drink's qualities to the public. But alas! After just a few years of service, "Old Doc" was retired prematurely, his jovial face no longer required. Seems he evoked a certain "medicinal" connotation. Courtesy Dr Pepper Company

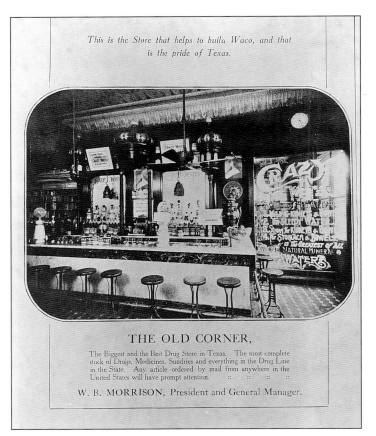

This is the Store that helps to build Waco, and that is the pride of Texas.

THE OLD CORNER,

The Biggest and the Best Drug Store in Texas. The most complete stock of Drugs, Medicines, Sundries and everything in the Drug Line in the State. Any article ordered by mail from anywhere in the United States will have prompt attention. :: :: ::

W. B. MORRISON, President and General Manager.

The Old Corner Drugstore
The Old Corner Drugstore was located on Fourth and Austin in the midst of bustling Waco, Texas. Owned and operated by W. B. Morrison, it dominated the social scene. The elaborate soda fountain area was the main attraction, serving numerous concoctions of the day. Town doctors, travelers, and cowboys mingled within its roomy interior, sharing stories, jokes, and refreshments. In November 1897, it became the site of a shoot-out between Judge G. B. Gerald and two newspapermen, apparently the result of a long time feud. But more important, The Old Corner Drugstore's historical status was secured when pharmacist Alderton developed the Dr Pepper formula. This photograph was taken when bottled "Crazy Water" was at the height of its popularity. The Texas Collection, Baylor University, Waco, Texas

Assuming its rightful place among the emerging roster of carbonated beverages, Dr Pepper has gone on to become one of the soft drink world's distinct flavors. Whether at 10, 2, or 4 o'clock, it's always in demand by thirsty pilots and passengers of America's automobiles.

Dr Pepper Neon Clock
The numerals 10, 2, and 4 reflect one of Dr Pepper's most successful advertising slogans. Research conducted at Columbia University revealed that these were the precise hours that an average person's energy level dropped. Because Dr Pepper contained inverted sugars readily absorbed by the bloodstream, it produced an immediate energy lift that counteracted this cycle. The slogan "Drink a Bite to Eat at 10, 2, and 4 o'clock" was introduced in 1926 and survived in one form or another for thirty years. Courtesy of the Dr Pepper Museum, Waco, Texas

ROEN'S A&W ROOT BEER

"A scaled-down mug was produced by the Indiana Glass Company during the early twenties. Designed exclusively for children, it held a 3 1/2 ounce squirt of root beer."

Miniature root beer mugs hardly seem like something substantial enough to build a business upon. Yet America's A&W Drive-Ins have managed to do just that, continuing today with their free flagon of drink for the toddlers. The curious tradition began during the early twenties, a few thousand gulps after chain founders Allen and Wright first teamed up to sell their sweet brew to California motorists.

Ted Roen's Ravenna, Ohio, Stand

Ted Roen fooled around with automobiles most of his life. Trouble was, his trio of A&W Drive-Ins took up so much of his time that he didn't have the opportunity to enjoy his hobby. For purely selfish reasons, he decided to start a regular "cruise-nite" at his Ravenna, Ohio, A&W stand in 1979. "If I couldn't be out with my friends, I decided to bring them to me." Now, he sees "a lot of gray hair" out there on the parking lot—along with flashy hot rods and souped-up vehicles. Every Wednesday night, automobile aficionados from fifteen county areas come to show-off their pride and joy. At Ted Roen's Ohio A&W, they still make food the way customers want it, use real carhops instead of electronic ordering boxes, and never serve root beer without a frosty mug. What's more, they don't take American Express.... Courtesy Ted Roen

From the start, serving youngsters with root beer was a daunting task. While kids loved the tasty drink, stealing swigs from a parent's tankard added nothing to their enjoyment. Still, what else could be done? Standard-sized mugs were simply too large for tiny hands. They were heavy, imposing, and prone to accidental spillage. What's more, the volume of liquid they contained was usually too great for the little ones. A smaller copy of the adult decanter was needed, one young moppets could polish off without parental assistance.

To the delight of juveniles and approval of parents, a scaled-down mug was produced by the Indiana Glass Company during the early twenties. Designed exclusively for children, it held a 3 1/2 ounce squirt of root beer—plenty for all those under six. Featuring a petit handle, fluted base, round dimples, and the familiar A&W logo embossed into the glass, it possessed all the characteristics of the larger version. Finally, tikes clamoring for refreshment in the backseat had their own container.

By the time young Lila Roen secured employment as an A&W carhop in Marshfield, Wisconsin, in 1942, the so-called "kiddy mug" promotion was already a long-established tradition. Eventually though, she married and left her work as a car server, but never forgot the friendly faces and happy times experienced in the business of roadside root beer.

When husband Vernon announced in the early fifties that he wanted more out of life than just a sales position for the Sears Company, they began their search for a profitable and enjoyable business venture. At the time, mutual friends already ran their own A&W franchise. Lila's fond memories of her early job experience were rekindled and their choice became clear. Is there doubt that she remembered the cute little mugs and cracked a smile?

In May of 1956, the Roens picked out three locations in the Ravenna, Ohio, area and proceeded to build their own network of A&W outlets. When all were completed in 1957, they became typical examples of the automobile drive-in, serving a simple menu of regular and foot-long hot dogs, root beer floats, barbecued beef, milkshakes, orange drinks, and popcorn. When son Ted and his wife Elma took over the operation in 1971, burgers became the favorite—but the little mugs were never forgotten. He continued the established traditions, his primary consideration to recruit an entirely new generation of root beer lovers.

Yet a measure of dedication was required for Roen to keep his liquid treat in the limelight. With only half the carbonation of the average soft drink, root beer must be served in a frigid container to maintain its fizz and froth; lukewarm glassware just won't do. A thick mug chilled in a deep freeze is the only container for the job. When served up properly, there's nothing that compares. "The kids know Coca-Cola and Pepsi," says Roen, "but they don't know root beer. When they finally do get a taste of it, they really like it!"

However, the simple secret behind Ted Roen's successful string of A&W

A&W Root Beer Patch
When Roy Allen and Frank Wright teamed up to sell root beer in the early twenties, they decided to combine their initials and form a new company name. A&W was the result, incorporated into a graphic symbol featuring the now-familiar "pointing arrow." From the Chuck Sturm Collection

A&W Kiddy Mug
Left, to the delight of juveniles and approval of parents, a scaled-down A&W mug was first produced by the Indiana Glass Company during the early twenties. Designed exclusively for children, it held a 3 1/2 ounce squirt of root beer, plenty for all those under six.

Drive-Ins lies not only in his zeal for developing new customers, but in his personal philosophy as well. "When it's done right, there is still room in the marketplace for the old-fashioned operator who wants to take care of his customers and give them good value," he suggests. "Not everything can come back again—but quality and taking care of the customer never dies."

In effect, that credo sums up the whole idea behind the notion of the little children's mug: making doubly sure that everyone, including the youngest members of every carload, exit the parking lot grinning from ear to ear, bellies filled with freshly brewed, delicious, ice-cold root beer. Ted Roen can be proud of his reputation for quality, because somewhere, somehow, Allen & Wright are smiling, too. ■

continued from page 166

Home, spied an extremely unusual coffee-shop called Googie's. Impressed by the design, he used the term in an article to classify the architectural forms of Coffee-shop Modern. Typified by gravity-defying abstracts, the Googie style combined multiple structural systems made up of materials like glass block, plastic, asbestos, cement, and plywood. Re-energized with these new components, the eye-popping arrangements that comprised the programmatic buildings of the twenties were retrofitted for the modern boulevard.

The coffee-shop became a dramatic roadside form: steel channel decking, neon tubing, delta wings, glass louvers, exposed support beams, terrazzo tile, and integrated billboards (sign as part of building) became a few of its hallmarks. As a consequence, drive-ins could no longer compete visually with extraordinary structures exemplified by Ship's, Biff's, Burke's, Coffee Dan's, Carolina Pines, Romeo's Times Square, or the Clock. On the West Coast, the future had arrived in the form of a coffee-shop, re-classifying dine-in-your-car curb service as a vestige of old.

Despite their impact on the drive-in trade, the modern coffee-shops had little effect on the monumental growth of the fast-food franchising industry. The reasons were obvious: by replicating established food and service systems already proven for their profitability, entrepreneurs could establish a suc-

Hart's Neon Burger Sign
Hart's 19¢ hamburger price started a price war with the Sacramento Stan's (visible in the background). Eventually, most of the burger joints throughout the states raised their prices, relegating the 15¢ hamburger to history. H. Sweet Collection, City of Sacramento, History and Science Division, Sacramento Archives and Museum Collection Center

When McDonald's announced in 1967 that it was going to increase the price of its hamburgers to eighteen cents, shock waves rocked the entire franchise industry; the average price of a burger had remained at fifteen cents for years. Labeled by the press as "Black Wednesday," the stage was set for the eventual elimination of many of the smaller hamburger chains.

Porky's Drive-In

St. Paul, Minnesota's famous Porky's Drive-In was shut down for many years in the 1980s, with broken neon glass covering the parking area and grass growing between cracks in the pavement. Owner Ray Truelson revived the classic drive-in in 1990 with drive-thru and walk-in service for the cars parking under the canopy. On any weekend night in the summer, owners of classic cars, hot rods, customs, and motorcycles make their pilgrimage to Porky's, overflowing from the parking lot to line both sides of University Avenue for a block in either direction. The action doesn't let up until the neon turns off after midnight.
Michael Dregni

cessful food enterprise quickly. As a bonus, advertising campaigns like those employed to market soap powder or aspirin ensured franchisees a steady supply of burger biters. The statistics didn't lie: by 1956, Ray Kroc had only thirteen McDonald's units in operation. Three years later, he boosted that figure to 100 franchise outlets nationwide. In 1959 alone, 67 new pairs of the bold yellow arches would light up strips across America.

Capitalizing on menu simplicity and task streamlining, a rash of imitators cloned their own versions of the McDonald's formula. A spontaneous race to spread the verisimilitude of the hamburger had begun. Originating in 1956 in Gary, Indiana, a new chain named after its founder's daughter attempted to mirror Kroc's success. Substituting turquoise boomerangs for the arches and promising "A serving a second," the Carrol's chain grew to over 163 units by the seventies. Sandy's, yet another McDonald's look-alike from Illinois, multiplied into a string of 250 during that same period. Proclaiming "Thrift and Swift Service," the chain's plaid-kilted Sandy proved that a little lass could sell a lot of hamburgers. In 1953, George E. Read's patented "Insta-Burger Broiler" also inspired Keith Cramer to open a walk-up based on the McDonald's model. When Hawaii hosted Cramer's 2,000th Burger King in 1977, the flame-broiled "Whopper" was already a mainland staple.

Suddenly, it seemed as if every splatter of grease on the grill was turning to gold. To the amazement of the food industry, even more self-serve copy cats decided to capitalize on the "cash cow," including Frank Thomas with Burger Chef restaurants and William Hardee with his Hardee's chain. A stampeding herd of competitors kept on a comin', including Biff's, Jiffy, Golden Point, Kelly's, Burger Queen, Henry's, Steer-In, Wetson's, Carter's, Burgerville USA, Mr. Fifteen, and Burger Boy Food-O-Rama. The roadsides became thick with cheap meat sandwiches in the round.

continued on page 183

Mels Drive-In
Today, a drive-in revival is bringing back former drive-ins and building new ones. Delighting visitors with their fantastic attractions, the Universal Studios theme parks in Hollywood, California and Orlando, Florida pay homage to the drive-in legacy begun by restauranteur Mel Weiss. Both locations feature an idealized re-creation of the now legendary Mels Drive-In. ©1992 Universal Studios Florida

Mels American Graffiti

*"With the drive-in as backdrop, customers related
their early years of love and romance—how they first met at Mels—
dated, and ultimately got married!"*

Tourists are generally unaware that along with the Golden Gate Bridge and its trolleys, San Francisco is famous for drive-ins. Mel Weiss and Harold Dobbs started it all back in 1947 when they built their first carhop eatery, inspired by similar restaurants serving motorists in Los Angeles. With a staff of fourteen carhops covering a 30,000 square foot parking lot, they lured the hungry with a local radio personality broadcasting a live remote. As music reverberated through car radios in the drive-ups, the curb-stepping gals of 140 South Van Ness became a new paradigm for service.

At all hours of the day and night, crowds of patrons that fancied dining-in-your-car came early and often. It didn't take long for the first unit to multiply into eleven! Six Mels became landmarks in the Bay Area with an additional cluster achieving their own notoriety in Stockton and Sacramento. They reigned for almost twenty years, until a parade of franchised fast food outlets finally outpaced their service. As the new philosophy of "serve yourself" began to reprogram attitudes about dining, Mels began its gradual decline.

By 1972, a New York restaurant conglomerate purchased most of the faltering units and changed their names. As colorful marquees were scheduled for removal, it appeared to many local enthusiasts that Mel's success story was about to end. They were only partly right. Around the same time, filmmaker George Lucas was scouting out locations to serve as centerpiece for his rock'n'roll fable about life, love, and coming of age in postwar America. The original Mels burger spot came to his attention and was leased prior to its demolition. Crews descended on the site and soon it was lights…camera…action…all over again. Mels was back in business, immortalized in 35mm.

Out on the parking lot, Ron Howard, Candy Clark, Richard Dreyfuss, Mackenzie Phillips, Harrison Ford, Cindy Williams, Paul LeMat, Suzanne Somers, and Charlie Martin Smith took their first steps to future stardom. As the bulldozers razed the last remnants of the historic drive-in and trucks carted off the debris, *American Graffiti* opened in theaters.

Thirteen years later, Mel's son Steven began to grow increasingly nostalgic about his father's defunct dream. As memories of the fifties dominated his imagination like a jukebox replaying the same old record, he tried to dismiss the thoughts. A lifetime of experience in the restaurant business told him that any attempt to resurrect the Mels idea wouldn't be easy. His father agreed, actively discouraging the idea. Fortunately, Steven persisted. When partner Donald Wagstaff confirmed interest with his own commitment, the path to reclaim a Northern California legend was clear.

At the grand re-opening in 1985, Steven's fondest wishes were realized: former teenagers who once dined at the first Mels were now re-visiting with their families. Weary of tasteless road food, they wanted to show their kids a glimpse of what the "good times" were really like—long before the age of video games and compact disc players. With the drive-in as backdrop, customers related their early years of love and romance—how they first met at Mels—dated, and ultimately got married! Mels was back on the charts with new locations on Frisco's Lombard and Gary Street. Two more opened in Los Angeles—joined by full-scale replicas (complete with food service) at the Universal Studios theme parks in Florida and California. Weiss had the Mels name officially trademarked in 1985 and now, it continues to take on a life of its own. Rightly so!

After all, Mels Drive-In is the burger, the French fry, and the milkshake. It's playing a joke on friends by unscrewing the top of the salt shaker and ketchup cap. Mels is the howlin', prowlin', Wolfman Jack…the phase-shift echo heard when walking past a row of roadsters tuned to the same raucous station. It's the haunting sound of an electric guitar banging out the "chunka-chunka" rhythm of "Green Onions" while cruisin' the circuit in a little deuce coupe, hair slicked back in a ducktail. Mels is the generic haven for the automobile, the youthful hangouts fondly remembered, along with one's first car, first date…and first kiss. ■

Mels Drive-In on South Van Ness

"Didn't we meet at Mels?" has become the popular slogan for the new chain of Mels restaurants operated by Steven Weiss and partner Donald Wagstaff in California. The original Mels Drive-In located at 140 South Van Ness in San Francisco was started in 1947 by Steven's father, Mel. After the movie American *Graffiti was filmed there during the early seventies, it was demolished. Fortunately, the film re-awakened interest in the idea of hanging out at the drive-in and the Mels concept was reborn for a new generation of diners.* Courtesy Steven Weiss

Mels Drive-In San Francisco
In 1985, Steven Weiss and partner Donald Wagstaff re-opened Mels Drive-In. Two new locations on Frisco's Lombard Street and Geary Boulevard attracted crowds, and classic cars. The fifties were back, complete with neon, hamburgers, chrome, and the milkshake! ©1994 Annabelle Breakey

Mels Salinas Drive-In

During the fifties, Mel Weiss operated a string of successful drive-in restaurants throughout California. His flagship San Francisco eatery was made famous by its appearance in the movie American Graffiti. The curb server classic depicted in this rare color image gained notoriety simply by supplying burgers and fries to the residents of Salinas. Most remembered by the high school crowd (it was only two blocks away) for its multi-colored curb-girl sign and distinctive "winged" architecture, it was eventually replaced by a Burger King. ©1955 Andy Southard, Jr.

Mels Drive-In Burger Pin

Left, Mels Drive-In restaurant and the classic sesame-seed bun hamburger: two inseparable institutions that have made this country worth fighting for. Pin Courtesy of Steven Weiss

continued from page 177

When the McDonald's Corporation announced in 1967 that it was going to increase the price of its hamburgers to eighteen cents, shock waves rocked the entire franchise industry; the average price of a burger had remained at fifteen cents for years. Blamed on rising beef costs and spiraling operating expenses, the meat hike was an ominous precursor to the great burger battles soon to come. Labeled by the press as "Black Wednesday," the stage was set for the eventual elimination of many of the smaller hamburger chains. After a period of unprecedented growth, the wild proliferation of the McDonald hamburger clones was over.

But what about the drive-ins? By the early eighties, the eat-in-the-front-seat format featuring carhops and serving trays was hardly mentioned! Sadly, the entire concept was regarded as impotent, unfit as a contender. When the Jack in the Box clown (who was part of a drive-thru intercom system) was detonated on national television, the pure form of the drive-in restaurant had already mutated into something unrecognizable. The unforgettable curb service eateries that captivated the imagination of an entire nation slipped into obscurity along with the services and features that made them great. With life quickening, motorists imagined themselves in too much of a hurry even to stop! Drive-thru windows (a method first tried in 1931 by the Pig Stands) and electronic menus became the norm.

Now, even the need to turn off the car motor was eliminated.

Fortunately, a few of the mom-and-pop operations continued to slog through the slush of burgers. Family-run landmarks like Atlanta's Varsity and Norfolk's Doumar's made a defiant stand against the franchising pods threatening to take away their souls.

Troy Smith managed to perpetuate his original drive-in chain and took the company to the operators in 1973. Sonic Industries was formed and true to name, they streaked towards success—indicated by the fact that 130 units were still operating! By the time C. Stephen Lynn became President and Chief Executive Officer in 1983, Sonic's number had grown to over 900 units. When Lynn and key management completed a leveraged buyout in 1986, Smith's original philosophy that "owners make better managers" helped rocket the organization to prominence. By 1994, Sonic became America's number one drive-in with over 1,300 units in operation.

With the introduction of their "Beach Burger '50s Combo" meal during the summer of 1990, Sonic helped fuel the nation's growing interest in nostalgia and the fifties. In thirty-second television ads, teen idol and *Beach Blanket Bingo* star Frankie Avalon pitched the new hamburger meal deal with assistance from Sue Phillips (winner of the company's 1989–1990 Carhop of the Year contest). In the spot, Avalon sat in a sandpile at one of Sonic's automotive stalls and entertained a daydream about the perfect day at the beach. Of course, his ultimate fantasy included the Beach Burger Combo.

For the millions of car-crazy Americans enamored of the drive-in restaurant's glory days, the timing of the commercial couldn't have been more appropriate. Classic car organizations and cruising clubs had begun seeing a marked increase in membership. As more and more baby boomers realized that the car could serve as a time machine, restoring the beautiful machines of yesteryear grew into a popular hobby. And naturally, this swelling body of street rodders required appropriate locations to display their pride and joy. Car shows were nice, but nothing equaled the drive-in as the ultimate location to park, cruise, and show off. To the delight of the few drive-ins remaining, the generation that fell in love with carhop service as teens had come full circle, rediscovering dining in your car by way of the internal-combustion engine.

continued on page 187

To the delight of the few drive-ins remaining, the generation that fell in love with carhop service as teens had come full circle, rediscovering dining in your car by way of the internal-combustion engine.

ROLLER SKATES ECHO THE AUTO

Joseph Merlin, a Belgian musical instrument craftsman and inventor, fashioned the world's first pair of roller skates around 1760. His enthusiasm for the gadget was demonstrated during a masquerade at Carlisle House (in the Soho Square district of London), where he glided among revelers, playing violin. Unfortunately, he misjudged his forward momentum and crashed headlong into a mirror, shattering interest in his wheels.

By the time Merlin recuperated from his injuries, a number of tinkers began improving his design. In 1819, Frenchman Monsieur Petitbled introduced the predecessor of today's inline blades by lining up a quartet of ivory wheels in a single row. Further refinement in 1823 by London fruit merchant Robert John Tyers resulted in skates that featured five aligned wheels—one of larger diameter in the center, employed as a turning pivot.

In a precursor of events to come, the proprietor of a Berlin beer tavern known as the Corse Halle encouraged its barmaids to strap on the wheeled contraptions in 1840. Laden with steins, buxom table servers soon scuttled about on roller skates, delivering their brew to thirsty customers. Service improved dramatically, albeit with mishaps: dodging tipsy customers proved difficult with rollers that tended to go straight.

Fortunately, that problem was somewhat alleviated in 1849, when Frenchman Louis Legrange split the inline wheels into two pairs. Fourteen years later, American James Plimpton contributed the missing link needed for ultimate maneuverability: a springy rubber mount. Now, by "rocking" the angle of the foot while in motion, two parallel sets of rollers could be influenced to execute a smooth skating curve.

With most of the bugs worked out, roller skating fell in and out of favor over the next seven decades, until the third major revival hit the nation during the thirties. In 1932, Olympic star Sonja Henie inspired movie-goers with her ice-skating prowess, further stimulating interest in the hobby. Suddenly, everyone who could afford inexpensive skate rental laced up, experiencing for themselves the wonders of roller skating.

Inspired by the growing interest, American industry saw the potential and outfitted employees with wheels. United Airlines experimented with strap-on rollers for their ticket agents and terminal workers. Western Union supplied skates to their message matrons, as did American Telephone and Telegraph. Operators skated through their work day, delivering messages, connecting customers.

It wasn't long before drive-in restaurants began experimenting with free-wheeling car service—pushing the idea of mobility to the extreme. Speed suddenly became an important factor of service, directly affecting customer satisfaction and turnover. To accommodate the pace, carhops had to cover ground as effortlessly as the vehicles on the boulevard. Miniaturized re-creations of tires, axles, and shock absorbers—mounted underfoot—became the ultimate means to mimic the movement of the motorcar.

Ultimately, the act of waitressing with tiny wheels strapped to one's feet proved too impractical. To become as graceful as one of Gloria Nord's Skating Vanities while balancing a loaded tray called for a marked level of skill and coordination. Even the most experienced skaters had problems, especially when they hit the gravel at the parking lot edge.

Though connected forever in the public's mind as standard equipment of the car server, roller skates were to be reserved exclusively for special promotions and publicity events. Served tray-top—shakes, burgers, and dogs were extremely popular with American car customers—but lost most of their appeal when abruptly deposited in one's lap. ∎

Courtesy Metro ImageBase

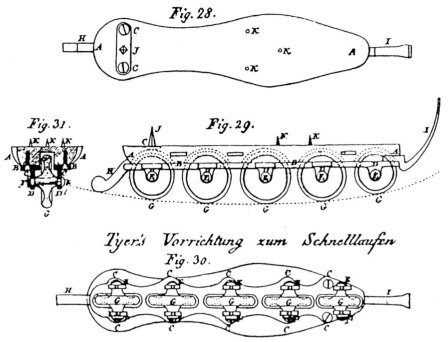

Roller Skate Patent Drawing

In 1823, London fruit merchant Robert John Tyers improved the roller skate with his own version. He called his model the "Volito" and fashioned the pair with a lineup of five wheels, the center roller having a larger diameter than the rest. The two wheels at the front and back were used for normal skating and the center spinner employed when turning. Today's "inline skates" are really nothing new—they have been around for centuries, predecessor to the carhop's working footwear.

American Graffiti Album

Left, roller-skate-riding carhops was more an image of drive-in folklore and myth than of reality and history. The image was made popular in the film American Graffiti, which played at movie theaters during the early 1970s. Later, it became a cult classic and is now replayed frequently on television. Ron Howard, Candy Clark, Richard Dreyfuss, Mackenzie Phillips, Harrison Ford, Cindy Williams, Paul LeMat, Suzanne Somers, and Charlie Martin Smith all took their first steps to future stardom in this drive-in classic. Album soundtrack circa 1973. David Willardson, cover artist. Copyright © by Universal City Studios, Inc. Courtesy of MCA Publishing Rights, a Division of MCA Inc.

RAMONA LONGPRÉ, MELS DRIVE-IN

Ramona Longpré was employed as a carhop at a number of California drive-in restaurants during the fifties and sixties. Her most memorable assignment: curb-girl at the Berkeley Mels. Although she never wore roller skates like the gals portrayed in the motion picture *American Graffiti*, she donned the smart service uniform and signature jacket that became the standard for West Coast car culture during the golden age of the drive-ins.

Sometimes, she would fill in for girls at a few of the other Mels locations, including the auto eatery many hops referred to as the "big stand" in San Francisco. But regardless of the particular locality, those nights spent serving the denizens of the roadways were pretty much the same: Fun food served up fast and furious in an atmosphere that reeked of pure excitement.

While toting trays at Mels, there was never a dull moment. She met lifelong friends there and wouldn't trade her experiences for anything. "Being a carhop at Mels was the best job I ever had," she proclaims proudly. "If I could do it again, I would!" When questioned further about the boundless energy most of today's retired curb-girls seem to exude, Ramona quickly explains why her associates seem so sprightly: "We have to be energetic…after all, we didn't save any of our money during our youth!" Today, Ramona operates a bar out in Point Richmond, California, and has permanently retired her window tray and ordering pad. ∎

continued from page 183

Now, as our nation heads towards the second millennium, "cruise nights" have become a common occurrence at remaining curb servers all across the country. In California, automobile clubs like the Auto Butchers, L.A. Roadsters, Over the Hill Gang, Road Kings, Rodfathers, West Coast Kustoms, and the Yakety-Yaks convene regularly at Bob's Big Boy in Toluca Lake (as of this writing, a landmark spared demolition). Sometimes, it's *American Graffiti* all over again when the clubs cruise Mels Drive-Ins. To everyone's approval, owner Steven Weiss has lovingly resurrected the fifties food bar with a quartet of outlets in Los Angeles, San Francisco, Sherman Oaks, and Woodland Hills. On special occasions, carhops return to duty as roadsters, woodies, and coupes rule the lot.

In the state where it all began, the same rituals are repeated. At the Pig Stand in Beaumont, Texas—perhaps the nation's oldest circular drive-in—"Eat a Pig Sandwich" continues as the popular slogan. Today, a new crowd of visitors eyeball the crazy rock and roll canopy and marvel at the neon pylons that wowed diners during the forties. Owner Richard Hailey hosts nostalgic festivities at the Broadway Pig Stand in San Antonio, including cruise nights frequented by the Best Little Ford Club in Texas, the Falcon Club, the Mopar Club, the Packard Club, and the T-Bird Club. At a recent event, local radio station KJ-97 staged a remote broadcast. A chauffeured ride in Elvis' black 1971 Caddy was a contest prize, and a dinner of Pig Sandwiches with all the trimmings was served to the winning couple.

In the Midwest, A&W Root Beer operator Ted Roen continues his own traditions in Ravenna, Ohio. Every Wednesday night during the summer months, his cooling refreshments are reserved for the local cruisers. Car organizations like the Nostalgic Cruisers and the Coachman Street Rod Club take over the grocery and drugstore's adjoining parking lots. A disc jockey spins stacks of wax from the fifties as revelers participate in a dance contest ("Come on baby, let's do the twist") and an entertaining trivia quiz. It's a blast from the past, fueled with mugs of frosty root beer.

Regardless of locality, the force that once contributed to the demise of the drive-in is now influencing its revival. While the unchanneled energies of youth may have caused trouble during the sixties, that exuberance has grown into experience and a respect for the way things were. Police patrols and entry gates are no longer needed. Ordinances have been discarded. Now, the baby-boom car crowd congregates to gather with friends, show off restored automobiles, and relive a few of the memories from the "good ol'days." Despite the passing years and changes, it's still a real "gas" to hop in a convertible, put the top down, and cruise to the nearest hamburger stand.

Fast food, step aside. The American drive-in restaurant—it's still as good as you remember! ∎

BIBLIOGRAPHY

"Add Sparkle…Add Profits…to Your Drive-In With Council Canopies!" *Drive-In Restaurant* (November-December 1961): 24.

"Air-Conditioned Drive-In Service." *American Restaurant* (July 1957): 69.

Allen, Jane E. "White Tower Eatery Becomes Museum Piece." *Sunday News Journal*, Wilmington, Delaware (January 3, 1988): B7.

Anderson, Warren H. *Vanishing Roadside America*. Tucson: The University of Arizona Press, 1981.

Anderson, Will. *Mid-Atlantic Roadside Delights*. Portland, Maine: Anderson & Sons Publishing Co., 1991.

Anderson, Will. *New England Roadside Delights*. Portland, Maine: Anderson & Sons Publishing Co., 1989.

"Announcing the Exciting Childers New Look For Drive-Ins." *Drive-In Restaurant* (February 1964): 29-33.

Anson, Mike. "Drive-In Ettiquette." *Motor Trend* (March 1989): 8.

Armour, Richard. *Drug Store Days: My Youth Among the Pills and Potions*. New York: McGraw-Hill Book Company, Inc., 1959

"A&W Shows New Designs." *Drive-In Restaurant* 32 (July 1968): 42-43.

"A Blast From the Past—Cafe an Explosion of Things '50s." *Identity* (Winter 1990): 28-31, 78.

"Always Beckoning Customers…the ABC's of Good Design." *American Restaurant Magazine* 40 (May 1957): 214-216.

"Aut-O-Hop Electronic Carhop Systems." *Drive-In* (June 1955): 14-15.

"Automobile Air Conditioners Send Sales Up 20%." *Fountain & Fast Food* (July 1955): 30-31.

Baeder, John. *Gas, Food, and Lodging: A Postcard Odyssey Through the Great American Roadside*. New York: Abbeville Press, 1982.

Baraban, Regina. "The Amazing Evolution of Fast Food." *Restaurant Design* (Winter 1981): 30-37.

Bailey, K.V. "The Silent Salesman." *The Diner* 7 (September 1948): 14.

"Better Drive-In Service with Functional Planning." *American Restaurant* 33 (September 1951): 59, 79.

"Big Business with Small Menu." *American Restaurant* 38 (July 1955): 86, 89.

Bigelow, John. "The Detroit Study of Drive-In Problems." *Drive-In Restaurant* (August 1964): 12-15.

"Bloomington Gets Beautiful Restaurant Theatre—The Phil-Kron." *American Restaurant Magazine* (October 1947):62-63, 96.

Boas, Max and Steve Chain. *Big Mac: The Unauthorized Story of McDonald's*. New York: E.P. Dutton and Co., Inc., 1976.

Bongiorno, Bill. "Cruising Nick's." *Hot Rod* (March 1989): 112.

Bottles, Scott L. *Los Angeles and the Automobile: The Making of a Modern City*. Los Angeles: University of California Press, 1987.

Boyne, Walter J. *Power Behind the Wheel: Creativity and Evolution of the Automobile*. New York: Stewart, Tabori & Chang, 1988.

Brown, William R. "The 'Teen' Problem." *Drive-In and Carryout* (August 1970): 27-30; (September 1970): 28-29, 49.

"Brooklawn Serves Cars At Fountain." *Fountain Service* (November 1947): 26-27.

"The Burger Queen." *Drive-In Restaurant* 27 (September 1963): 16-19.

Burroughs, A. D. "First Impressions Are Lasting Impressions…." *Drive-In Restaurant and Highway Cafe Magazine* 20 (March 1956): 8.

"The Butterfly." *Drive-In Restaurant and Highway Cafe Magazine* 19 (July 1955): 15.

Caldwell, Bruce; Editor. *Petersen's The Best of Hot Rod*. Los Angeles, California: Petersen Magazine Network, 1986.

Califano, Alfred N. "A Study of Curb Service Drive-In Restaurants." *Drive-In Restaurant* (July 1964): 13-15.

Campbell, Dana Adkins. "Yesterday's Sodas and Shakes." *Southern Living* 27 (February 1992): 130.

"Canopies: What's Behind an old Standby's New Appeal." *National Petroleum News* 50 (November 1958): 99-104.

"Carhop Orders Speeded By Walkie-Talkie." *Popular Mechanics.* (November 1951): 227.

Carlino, Bill. "Beach Blanket Burgers' Welcome Summer at Sonic." *Nation's Restaurant News* 24 (June 1990): 12.

"The Carvel Story." *Ice Cream Trade Journal* (March 1954): 26 and 28, 119-120.

Cass, Lionel E. "Drive-Ins Coming For British Highways." *Drive-In Restaurant and Highway Cafe* (January 1957): 10.

Cather, Eddie. "Thanks, Eddie." *Car and Driver* 37 (October 1991): 22.

Cawthorne, Nigel. *Sixties Sourcebook, A Visual Reference to the Style of a New Generation*. Secaucus, New Jersey: Chartwell Books, 1989.

Chazanov, Mathis. "A Burger To Go and a Landmark Drive-In Is Gone." *Los Angeles Times* (March 12, 1984): Metro, 1.

"Chicken In the Rough." *American Restaurant* (June 1958): 60-61.

Childs, Leslie. "Hot Dog Kennels' as Nuisances to Adjoining Property Owners." *American City* 63 (February 1928): 137.

"Circular Drive-In Includes Commissary." *Architectural Record* (September 1946): 101.

Claudy, C. H. "Organizing the Wayside Tea House." *Country Life in America* 29 (June 1916): 54.

"Clean-Ups Every Hour At Starlite Drive-In." *Fountain Service* (October 1947): 32-33.

"Clowns On Roller Skates—Carhops With Extra Appeal." *American Restaurant* (September 1954): 63.

Cody, Larch. "Are Drive-Ins Being Driven Out?" *Los Angeles Herald-Examiner* (March 4, 1973) California Living: 9-10.

"Coffee Drinking In Public Declines 22 Per Cent." *Drive-In Restaurant and Highway Cafe* (July 1955): 14.

Coleman, Brent. "Designing an Image, Businesses Want Competitive Distinction." *The Sacramento Union* (August 25, 1987) Business Tuesday: 1, 4-5.

"Colossal Drive-In For Super Scenery." *Architectural Record* (September 1946): 104.

Corwin, Miles and Lorna Fernandes. "They Voted to Preserve 43-Year Old Restaurant." *Los Angeles Times* (March 15, 1992): Section R.

Coyle, Patrick L. *The World Encyclopedia of Food*. New York: Facts on File, Inc., 1981.

Dawson, Jim and Steve Propes. *What Was the First Rock'n'Roll Record*? Boston: Faber and Faber, 1992.

"Designed to Stop Both Eye and Car." *Drive-In Restaurant* 25 (July 1961): 8-9.

"Delores Drive-In." *Nation's Restaurant News* (October 20, 1980): 18.

"A Detour for Roadside America." *Business Week* (February 16, 1974): 44.

"The Detroit Study of Drive-In Problems." *Drive-In Restaurant* (August 1964): 12.

Dettelbach, Cynthia Golomb. *In the Driver's Seat: The Automobile in American Literature and Popular Culture*. Westport, Connecticut: Greenwood Press, 1976.

DeWolf, Rose. "Ice Cream Sun Days, The Treat That Says Summer Drips With Delicious Memories." *New Choices For the Best Years* 30 (July 1990): 96.

Dickson, Paul. *The Great American Ice Cream Book*. New York: Atheneum, 1972.

"Dina-A-Mike." *Drive-In Restaurant* (November-December 1961): 25.

"Dogs and Suds." *American Restaurant* (June 1958): 63.

Dolan, Carrie. "If You Really Cut the Mustard, You Will Relish This Job." *The Wall Street Journal* (July 7, 1992): A1, A8.

"Doumar's Cones and Barbecue." *The Virginian* (August 1985).

"Drive-In Closes Curb Because of Rowdyism." *Drive-In Restaurant* (January 1964): 27.

"The Drive-In Ordinance and You." *Drive-In Restaurant* (February 1965): 26-27.

"Drive-In Ordinance Roundup." *Drive-In Restaurant* (November 1965): 22-23, 26; (August 1967): 39-41; (June 1967): 59.

"Drive-In Patios." *Drive-In Restaurant* (August 1963): 20-21.

"Drive-In Restaurant." *The Architectural Forum* (November 1945): 162-163.

"Drive-In Restaurant Near Jantzen Beach, Oregon." *Progressive Architecture* (June 1947): 61-63.

"Drive-In Restaurants and Luncheonettes." *Architectural Record* (September 1946): 99-106.

"Drive-In Restaurant Telephones." *Fountain Service* (July 1950): 28-29.

"Drive-In Service Goes Automatic." *American Restaurant* (September 1953): 89.

"The 'Drive-Thru.'" *Drive-In Restaurant and Highway Cafe* 21 (January 1957): 11.

Duffy, Tom. "Home of the Hamburger." *Celebration* Booklet; Seymour, Wisconsin (August 5, 1989): 1-7.

Dunne, Mike. "Can the Fab Fifties Rock 'n' Roll?" *The Sacramento Bee* Final (September 3, 1987) Scene and Style: 1, 6-7.

"Eating Goes On Assembly Line at California Drive-In." *Business Week* (July 23, 1949): 22-23.

"The Eccentric." *Drive-In Restaurant* 27 (November 1963): 31.

Eiss, Albert. "Carhop Service—Yes Or No?" *Restaurant Management* (June 1960): 32, 130, 132.

"1,800 Meals Is Daily Average at Steak n Shake, St. Louis, Mo." *Fountain and Fast Food* (September 1953): 50-51.

"The Electronic Ordering Systems Manufacturers Speak." *Drive-In* (April 1957): 5-15.

"Elevating the Standing of the 'Hot Dog Kennel'." *American City* 38 (May 1928): 99-100.

Ellis, Harry E. *Dr Pepper, King of Beverages*. Dallas, Texas: Taylor Publishing Company, 1979.

Emerson, Robert L. *Fast Food: The Endless Shakeout*. New York: Lebhar-Friedman, Inc., 1979.

"Everything is Automated But the Carhop." *Science Digest* (November 1966): 32.

Fair, Ernest W. "Denver…Where Business is Averaging $650,000 a Month For Restaurants." *American Restaurants* (August 1947): 24.

Fair, Ernest W. "Salt Lake City, A Great City for Eating Out and Keen Competition." *American Restaurant* (September 1947): 26-28, 66.

Fair, Ernest W. "Tulsa, One of the Best Restaurant Towns In The Nation…Where Drive-Ins Are Numerous and Sumptuous Dining Rooms Are the Rule." *American Restaurant* (May 1948): 30-32.

Fair, Ernest W. "Atlanta, Restaurants Are Doing a $20,000,000 Business in This Southern Metropolis." *American Restaurant* (May 1947): 22, 26, 52-53.

Fanald, Lon. "A Robot Takes the Car Hop Out of the Track's Service." *Fountain Service* (November 1950): 30.

Farragher, Marcella. "Graphics Splash Color Into Bland Buildings, Dunlavey Studio Pulls 3D Building Into Sharp Focus." *The Sacramento Union* (July 9, 1989) Home & Real Estate: 27, 29.

Farb, Peter and George Armelagos. *Consuming Passions: The Anthropology of Eating*. New York: Houghton Mifflin Company, 1980.

Ferguson, Frank L. *Efficient Drug Store Management*. New York: Fairchild Publications, Inc., 1969.

"50 Ideas For Drive-Ins." *American Restaurant* 42 (July 1959): 52-53, 86.

Finch, Christopher. *Highways to Heaven: The Auto Biography of America*. New York: HarperCollins Publishers, Inc., 1992.

"41 In Florida." *Drive-In Restaurant and Highway Cafe* (June 1955): 19, 26.

Fling, Ray. "Is the Public Turning Away From 'Established' Restaurants?" *Restaurant Management* (March 1929): 43-44.

Flink, James J. *The Automobile Age*. Cambridge, Massachusetts: The M.I.T. Press, 1988.

"Foods Made Fast Sell Fast." *American Restaurant* (February 1955): 70.

Franks, Julia. "California Dreaming." *Restaurant/Hotel Design International* (November 1989): 69, 71.

Frazer, Elizabeth. "The Destruction of Rural America: Game, Fish and Flower Hogs." *The Saturday Evening Post* (9 May, 1929): 39, 193-194, 197-198.

Friddel, Guy. "The Smithsonian Agrees: Doumar's Ice Cream Cone Was the First." *The Virginia Pilot* (March 18, 1994).

Furniss, Ruth MacFarland. "The Ways of the Tea House." *Tea Room Management* 1 (August 1922): 5.

Gaines, Jerry. "How We Handled the Kansas City Problem." *Drive-In Restaurant* (March 1965): 27.

Gebhard, David, and Harriette Von Breton. *L.A. in the Thirties*. New York: Peregrine Smith, Inc., 1975.

Gelderman, Carol. *Henry Ford, The Wayward Capilist*. New York: St. Martin's Press, 1981.

"Goodbye Carhops." *Fast Food* (November 1963): 18-21.

"Good Mormons Don't Go Broke." *Saturday Evening Post* (June 10, 1950): 48-49, 157-160.

Gordy, Wilbur Fisk. *History of the United States*. New York: Charles Scribner's Sons, 1922.

Goydon, Raymond. "Custard's Last Stand." *Forbes Magazine* (July 1, 1985).

Gutman, Richard J. S.; Kauffman, Elliot; and David Slovic. *American Diner*. New York: Harper & Row, 1979.

Gutman, Richard J. S. *American Diner, Then and Now*. New York: HarperCollins Publishers, Inc., 1993.

Hayes, Jack. "Drive-thrus Get Into the Fast Lane: Upstart 'Burger Boxes' Challenge Fast-Food Giants." *Nation's Restaurant News* 23 (November 1989): 1, 70.

Hastings, Charles Warren. "Roadtown, The Linear City." *Architects and Builders Magazine* 10 (August 1910): 445.

Heat Moon, William Least. *Blue Highways: A Journey Into America*. Boston: Atlantic Monthly Press, 1982.

Heimann, Jim and Rip Georges. *California Crazy, Roadside Vernacular Architecture*. San Francisco: Chronicle Books, 1980.

Helen Christine Bennett, "'Pinkie's Pantry' Took The Cake." *American Magazine* (June 1928): 65-66.

Hellemans, Alexander and Bryan Bunch. *The Timetables of Science*. New York: Simon and Schuster, 1988.

"Here's How Ott's Picks Good Dispensers." *Fountain Service* (January 1950): 32-33.

Hempt, Grace Elizabeth. "Old Grist Mill is Now a Tea Room." *Tea Room and Gift Shop* 2 (March 1923): 7.

Hess, Alan. *Googie, Fifties Coffee Shop Architecture*. San Francisco: Chronicle Books, 1985.

Hicks, Clifford B. "Computerburger Hit the Assembly Line." *Popular Mechanics* (September 1966): 81-85.

"Highway Restaurants" *Architectural Record* (October 1954): 163, 167-169.

Higdon, Edna. "Customers Phone the Orders At Bill's Seattle Drive-In." *Fountain Service* (November 1950): 31.

Hill, Debra Goldstein. *Price Guide to Coca-Cola Collectibles*. Lombard, Illinois: Wallace-Homestead Book Company, 1984.

Hirschman, Bill. "Confrontation Outside Drive-through Window Cost Man His Life." *The Wichita Eagle* (April 15, 1993) 1D, 3D.

Hirshorn, Paul and Stephen Izenour. *White Towers*. Cambridge, Massachusetts: The MIT Press, 1979.

Hoopes, Lydia Clawson. "From Root Beer Stand to Millions." *American Restaurant* 31 (May 1948): 39-42, 117-122.

"Houston's Drive-In Trade Gets Girl Show With Its Hamburgers." *Life* (February 26, 1940): 84-87.

"The Howard Johnson's Restaurants." *Fortune* 22 (September 1940): 82-87, 94, 96.

"How Drive-Ins Compare With Other Restaurants." *Drive-In Restaurant* 32 (April 1968): 40.

"How Pig Stands Started the Drive-In Restaurant." *Drive-In Management* (September 1961): 22-30.

Hungerford, Edward. "America Awheel." *Everybody's Magazine* 36 (June 1917): 678.

Hunt, Gordon. "Call the Mayor, They're Cruising Again!" *Drive-In Restaurant* (November 1965): 18-22.

Hunt, Mary. "Good-by To Everett's." *Ann Arbor Observer* 3-10 (June 1979): 27-28, 50.

Huxtable, Ada Louise. "Architecture for a Fast Food Culture." *New York Times Magazine* (February 12 1978): 23-25.

"Improve Your Service With Half The Help." *American Restaurant Magazine* (May 1955): 39.

"In Atlanta, All Roads Lead to the Varsity." *Business Week* 8 (October 1966): 132-133.

"In-Car 'Hopless' Service is Big Boy's Answer." *Fountain & Fast Food Service* (February 1952): 34.

Ingram, E.W., Sr. *All This From a 5-cent Hamburger! The Story of the White Castle System.* New York: The Newcomen Society in North America, 1964.

Jackson, Howard E. "It Pays to Pay Employees for Putting Forth Extra Effort." *American Restaurant* (June 1950): 35, 121.

Jarvis, Jack. "Tombstones To 'Burgers." *Seattle Post Intelligencer* (August 31, 1965).

Johnson, Robert. "Frozen Custard Is Soft Ice Cream But Hard To Find." *The Wall Street Journal* (June 19, 1986).

Jones, Dwayne and Roni Morales. "Pig Stands, The Beginning of the Drive-In Restaurant." *SCA NewJournal* 12 (Winter 1991-92): 2-5.

Jones, W.E. "A Million $ A Year, Allen's Drive-In Does It by Specializing, by Service, by Food Control, by Quality." *Fountain & Fast Food Service* (December 1951): 18.

Joy, Dena. "At the Car Hop, Drive-In Has Disappeared But Memories Remain for the Girls From Stan's." *The Bakersfield Californian* (March 11, 1986) Accent: 1-2.

Keegan, Peter O. "Video Drive-Thrus Speed Fast-Food Service." *Nation's Restaurant News* 24 (November 1990): 3, 110.

Keller, Ulrich. *The Highway as Habitat: A Roy Stryker Documentation, 1943-1955.* Santa Barbara, California: University Art Museum, 1986.

Kimball, Jim. "How Kim's Design Discourages Litterbugs." *Drive-In Restaurant* (November 1965): 27-29.

King, Marsha. "Cruising In the Past Lane." *Seattle Post Intelligencer* (June 14, 1992): Section K1-2.

Kendall, Elaine. "The Most Famous Boring Food In America." *Vogue* (October 1, 1969): 258, 260-261, 265.

"Kitchen Layout and Equipment Design Gives Fast Service at Hardee's." *Drive-In Restaurant* 26 (August 1962): 10-12.

Knutson, L.W. "Ideas From 20 Years in Drive-Ins." *Drive-In Restaurant* 30 (April 1966): 37-38, 67.

Kowinski, William Severini. "Suburbia: End of the Golden Age." *The New York Times Magazine* (16 March, 1980): 16-19, 106.

Kroc, Ray. *Grinding It Out: The Making of McDonald's.* Chicago, Illinois: Henry Regnery Company, 1977.

Kurtz, Stephen A. *Wasteland: Building the American Dream.* New York: Praeger Publishers, 1973.

Langdon, Philip. *Orange Roofs, Golden Arches: The Architecture of American Chain Restaurants.* New York: Alfred A. Knopf, 1986.

Lay, Charles Downing. "New Towns for High-Speed Roads." *Architectural Record* 78 (November 1935): 352-354.

Lewis, David L. and Lawrence Goldstein. *The Automobile and American Culture.* Ann Arbor: The University of Michigan Press, 1980.

Liebs, Chester. *Main Street to Miracle Mile: American Roadside Architecture.* Boston: Little, Brown & Co., 1985.

"Life After Death Along Gasoline Alley." *Fortune* (November 5, 1979): 86-89.

Linder, Robert. "Parking Comments." *Drive-In Restaurant* (March 1963): 20-22.

"Los Angeles Lowdown." *The Diner* (September 1946): 8-9.

Louis, David. *2201 Fascinating Facts.* New York: Wings Books, 1983.

Love, John F. *McDonald's: Behind the Arches.* New York: Bantam Books, 1986.

"Lunch Wagons Streamline—Customers Stream In." *Nation's Business* 25 (September 1937): 74.

Luxenberg, Stan. *Roadside Empires: How the Chains Franchised America.* New York: Viking Penguin, Inc., 1985.

Mackaye, Benton, and Lewis Mumford. "Townless Highways for the Motorist." *Harper's* 163 (August 1931): 347-356.

"Main Street 1910." *Fast Service* 39 (October 1980): 34-36, 61.

"Making Big Money For Owners!" *Fountain Service* (May 1948): 3.

Mariani, John. *America Eats Out.* New York: William Morrow and Company, Inc., 1991.

Marken, Cal. "How Big Are You?" *Drive-In Restaurant* (September 1965): 10.

Marks, David. "'A Dessert No Less Curious,' A Short History of Ice Cream in America." *Early American Life* 22 (June 1991): 64.

Markstein, David. "The Frostop Story." *Fountain and Fast Food* (September 1956): 56 and 58.

Marling, Karal Ann. *The Colossus of Roads: Myth and Symbol Along the American Highway.* Minneapolis: Univ. of Minnesota Press, 1984.

Martin, Richard. "Marriott Brings Car Hop Service to Bob's Big Boy." *Nation's Restaurant News* 24 (October 1990): 4.

Marvel, Bill. "Savoring the Classic Sizzle." *Dallas Times Herald* (August 26, 1984): 1E and 8E.

Matteson, Donald W. *The Auto Radio, A Romantic Genealogy.* Jackson, Michigan: Thornridge Publishing, 1987.

McCall, Bruce. "Los Angeles, Once Upon a Time." *The New Yorker* 67 (June 1991): 36.

"Mexican Foods—Family Style." *Drive-In & Carry-Out* (April 1969): 46-47.

"The Moderne." *Drive-In Restaurant and Highway Cafe Magazine* (October 1956): 19.

Montagne, Prosper. *Larousse Gastronomique.* New York: Crown Publishers, 1961.

"More Than a Shade of Difference." *Drive-In Restaurant* (November 1965): 16-17.

Morrison, Tom. *Root Beer Advertising and Collectibles.* West Chester, Pennsylvania: Schiffer Publishing, Ltd., 1992.

"Motormat 'Magic' a Revolutionary Method of Food Service For Drive-Ins." *American Restaurant* (September 1949): 48, 62.

"The New Outlet—Roadside Refreshment Stands." *Printer's Ink* 135 (22 April 1926): 127.

"New Profit Boom In Electronic Service." *Drive-In Restaurant and Highway Cafe* (November 1955): 12-14, 17.

"The Newspaper Said…Bill Ihlenfeldt Replied." *Drive-In Restaurant* (March 1965):26-27.

"Now! Only Aut-O-Hop Has AMG!" *Drive-In* (May 1958): 9.

"OK, Who Ordered the Burger With 500 Pickles?" *Life* (August 27, 1971): 68.

Oliver, Thomas. *The Real Coke, the Real Story.* New York, New York: Random House, 1986.

O'Meara, John B. "Drive-In Service Do's and Don'ts." *American Restaurant* 39 (July 1956): 70-71, 110-111.

O'Meara, John B. "Do's and Don'ts for Better Drive-In Service." *American Restaurant* 39 (July 1957): 82-85.

"122 Ideas For Drive-Ins." *American Restaurant* (June 1955): 65.

"One Million Hamburgers and 160 Tons of French Fries a Year." *American Restaurant* (July 1952): 44-45.

Oppel, Frank. *Motoring In America: The Early Years.* Secaucus, New Jersey: Castle Books, 1989.

Orth, Fred A. "Neon Gas Signs—What Are They?" *The American Restaurant* (April 1928): 53, 87-91.

Paul, John R. and Paul W. Parmalee. *Soft Drink Bottling, A History With Special Reference to Illinois.* Springfield: Illinois State Museum Society, 1973.

"Palaces of the Hot Doges." *Architectural Forum* 63 (August 1935): 30-31.

Patton, Phil. *Open Road: A Celebration of the American Highway.* New York: Simon & Schuster, 1986.

Pearce, Christopher. *Fifties Sourcebook, A Visual Guide to the Style of a Decade.* Secaucus, New Jersey: Chartwell Books, 1990.

Petretti, Allan. *Petretti's Coca-Cola Collectibles Price Guide.* Radnor, Pennsylvania: Wallace Homestead, 1992.

"Pick a Good Location." *American Restaurant Magazine* (October 1954): 71-73.

"Pizza Burger—New Idea In Sandwiches." *American Restaurant* (September 1954): 59.

"Prizes Mark Gala Opening." *Drive-In Restaurant and Highway Cafe* (August 1955): 5.

Poling-Kempes, Lesley. *The Harvey Girls, Women Who Opened the West.* New York: Paragon House, 1991.

Pollexfen, Jack. "Don't Get Out." *Collier's* (March 19, 1938): 18, 52-54.

Pomeroy, Ralph. *The Ice Cream Connection.* New York: Paddington Press, Ltd., 1975.

"Ptomaine Joe's Place." *Collier's* 102 (1 October 1938): 54.

"Puritan Maid Drive-Ins Feature Bird-In-Hand." *American Restaurant* (July 1940): 22.

Rapoport, Roger. "Restored Soda Fountains of Yesterday." *Americana* 19 (July-August 1991): 60-61, 64.

"Rectangular Drive-In With Non-Glare Front." *The Architectural Record* (September 1946): 103.

Reddin, John J. "Dag's Keeps Frying With Imagination." *Seattle Times* (April 15, 1962).

Reinhart, Dorothy. "Laughter, Tears Mark the Final Closing of Henry's, 41-Year Glendale Landmark." *The Ledger*, Glendale-Burbank (November 2, 1977): Section 3, 11.

Richmond, Ray. "Going, Going, Gone—It's Over For Tiny Naylor's" *Los Angeles Daily News* (March 14, 1984): L.A. Life, 7.

Riley, Robert M. "The Big Boom Out West: Coffee Shops." *Drive-In* (November 1961): 44-48.

"Roadside Diners." *The Architectural Record* (July 1934): 56-57.

"The Roadside Stand Grows Up—Ultra Modern, Magnificent." *Drive-In Restaurant and Highway Cafe Magazine* (November 1955): 21, 27.

"Robert C. Wian, Jr." *American Restaurant* (June 1952): 148.

Roberts-Dominguez, Jan. *The Mustard Book.* New York: Macmillan Publishing Company, 1993.

Rodd, W.C. "One Building For Two Types of Clientele." *American Restaurant Magazine* (August 1948): 35-37, 131.

"Roy W. Allen, Drive-In Pioneer, Dies at 85." *Drive-In Restaurant* (May 1968): 58-59.

Rubin, Charles J., David Rollert, John Farago, and Jonathan Etra. *Junk Food.* New York: Dell Publishing Co., Inc., 1980.

"Rutherford's Pioneer Drive-In Marks Thirty Years As Renton Institution." *Renton News Record* (April 11, 1960).

Sacharow, Stanley. *Symbols of Trade.* New York, New York: Art Direction Book Company, 1982.

"San Bernadino's New Drive-In Ordinance." *Drive-In Restaurant* (November 1964): 20-21.

Sare, John. "Unique Drive-In Recalled, Owner J.D. Sivils Has Died at Age 78." *Dallas Morning News* (June 24, 1986): 14A.

Schuman, Michael A. "A Trip Into the McPast." *The Seattle Times* (June 20, 1989): D6-7.

Segrave, Kerry. *Drive-in Theaters, A History From Their Inception In 1933.* Jefferson, North Carolina: McFarland & Company, Inc., Publishers, 1992.

"Selby Industries, Inc." *Drive-In Restaurant* (October 1963): 12.

Selby, John. "Prefab Canopies, The New Look in Drive-Ins." *Drive-In* (April 1958): 16-17.

"Service Fone Equipment." *Drive-In Restaurant* (February 1966): 51.

"Serving 3,000 Cars Daily." *American Restaurant Magazine* (August 1951): 42-43, 72.

"$64 Answers." *Drive-In Restaurant and Highway Cafe* (June 1955): 24, 27.

Skellenger, Gordon. "We Thought Everything Would Be All Right." *Drive-In Restaurant* (June 1965): 12.

Skenazy, Lenore. "The King Had a Love Affair With Food." *The Arizona Daily Star* (August 8, 1993): Section D, 11.

Short, Robert. "Delay Costs Man His Life at Restaurant." *Wichita Eagle* (April 14, 1993).

"Shrine To the Hamburger." *Popular Mechanics* (January 1949): 101-103.

Silk, Gerald, Angelo Anselmi, Henry Robert, Jr., and Strother MacMinn. *Automobile and Culture.* New York: Harry N. Abrams, Inc., 1984.

Snow, Richard F. "King Cone." *Invention & Technology* 9 (Fall 1993): 4-5.

Snyder, James. "Roadside Beauty and YOU." *Drive-In Restaurant* (November 1965): 24-26.

Society for Commercial Archeology. *The Automobile in Design and Culture.* Edited by Jan Jennings. Ames: Iowa State University Press, 1990.

Squire, Latham C., and Howard M. Bassett. "A New Type of Thoroughfare: The 'Freeway.'" *American City* 47 (November 1932): 64-66.

Steingarten, Jeffrey. "Simply Red." *Vogue* 182 (August 1992): 244, 298-300.

Stern, Jane and Michael Stern. *A Taste of America.* New York: Andrews and McMeel, 1988.

Stern, Jane and Michael Stern. *Encyclopedia of Pop Culture.* New York: HarperCollins Publishers, Inc., 1992.

Stern, Jane and Michael Stern. *RoadFood.* New York: HarperCollins Publishers, Inc., 1992.

Stern, Rudi. *Let There Be Neon.* New York: Harry N. Abrams, Inc., 1979.

Stuckey, Lillie and Avanelle Day. *The Spice Cook Book.* New York: David White Company, 1964.

"The Sweep Inn." *Drive-In Restaurant and Highway Cafe* (September 1955): 15.

Tackett, John. "Restaurant Wins Pig Sandwich Case." *The San Antonio Light* (February 16, 1990).

"Take Home Takes Up Slack In Volume." *American Restaurant Magazine* (April 1955): 92

Teague, Walter Dorwin. *Design This Day: The Technique of Order in the Machine Age.* New York: Harcourt, Brace & Co., 1940.

"A $10 Million Drive-In." *Drive-In Restaurant* (May 1964): 12-16.

Tennyson, Jeffrey. *Hamburger Heaven, The Illustrated History of the Hamburger.* New York: Hyperion, 1993.

"That's The Important Word—Thank You!" *Drive-In Restaurant* (October 1963): 12-13.

Thomas, Frank B. "Parking Comments." *Drive-In Restaurant* (March 1963): 21.

Thurow, Roger. "Frankly, Viennese Eschew Verbal Link to Their Weiners." *The Wall Street Journal* (February 15, 1994): A1, col. 4.

"Tomorrow's Secret of Faster Food Service." *American Restaurant Hospitality* (April 1963): 58.

Trap, Jack. *Roller Skating Start to Finish.* New York: Penguin, 1980.

"Tray on a Trestle Serves at Drive-In." *Popular Mechanics* 72 (September 1949): 127.

"2,500,000 gallons of Mix For Soft-Serve Products Sold By Tastee-Freeze in 1952." *Ice Cream Trade Journal* (July 1953): 38 and 79.

"2 'Catchy' Items…33 Busy Drive-Ins." *American Restaurant* (July 1958): 51.

"Two Roadside Drive-Ins Use Light Framing and Lots of Glass." *The Architectural Forum* (October 1946): 144.

"Unique Building Attracts Customers." *Soda Fountain* (September 1941): 58.

"Visual Attraction of Canopy Can Draw More Customers." *Drive-In* (April 1959): 34.

"Walkie-Talkie Drive-In." *Restaurant Management* (September 1951): 40-41, 103.

"Washington, D.C.: Curb-Service Dictates A New Form." *Architectural Record* (March 1938): 70-71.

Watters, Pat. *Coca-Cola, An Illustrated History.* New York: Doubleday & Company, Inc., 1978.

"Wayside Stands, Billboards, Curb Pumps, Lunch Wagons, Junk Yards, and Their Ilk." *American City* 44 (April 1931): 104-108.

Weinstein, Jeff. "Four Time-Worn Chains Plot Course For Recovery." *Restaurants & Institutions* 101 (November 1991): 39.

Welch, Dr. John M. "Is Experience and Asset of a Liability?" *Drive-In Restaurant* (April 1966): 39-40.

"Where the Drive-Ins Are." *Drive-In Restaurant* 28 (April 1964): 16.

"Who'll Get Helped or Hurt by Auto Freeways." *U.S. News and World Report* (21 December 1956):90-92.

Wilkins, Mike; Ken Smith and Doug Kirby. *The New Updated and Expanded Roadside America.* New York: Simon & Schuster, 1986.

William Poundstone. *Big Secrets, The Uncensored Truth About All Sorts of Stuff You Are Never Supposed to Know.* New York: William Morrow & Company, Inc., 1983.

Willis, Lyn. "J.A. Rutherford, Who Came West To Ranch, Eventually Struck Gold In the Northwest's First Drive-In Root Beer Stands." *Montana* 13 (Winter 1963): 8-17.

Wilson, Richard Guy; Dianne H. Pilgrim and Dickran Tashjian. *The Machine Age in America 1918-1941.* New York: Harry N. Abrams, Inc., 1986.

Witzel, Michael Karl. *The American Gas Station: History and Folklore of the Gas Station In American Car Culture.* Osceola, Wisconsin: Motorbooks International, 1992.

Woodson, LeRoy. *Roadside Food.* New York: Stewart, Tabori & Chang, Inc., 1986.

Wynne, Robert. "Hamming It Up, Pig Stands Mark 68th Year With '50s-Style Sock Hop." *The San Antonio Light* (October 12, 1989):F1, F17.

The World Book Encyclopedia. Chicago: Field Enterprises Educational Corporation, 1969.

"Your Curb is Your Atmosphere." *Drive-In Magazine* 24 (March 1960): 32-35.

INDEX

A&W Root Beer, 30-33, 65-73, 152, 172-173
Ace Foods (Milwaukee, WI), 137
Air conditioning, 126-127
Airdrome (San Bernardino, CA), 34-35, 37,
Alderton, Charles, 168-170
Allen, Roy W., 30-33
American Graffiti, 139, 178, 185
Anderson, Walter, 48-55
Anthony, Earl, 80
Arby's, 64
Avalon, Frankie, 183
Avayou, David, 112
Bart's Drive-In (Portland, OR), 46-48
Belt, A. H. "Gus," 161
Bennett, Mrs. Edwin, 128
Big Mac, 60-63
Bishop's Driv-Inn (Tulsa, OK), 100
Blackie's Drive-In (Chelsea, CT), 40-41
Bob's Big Boy, 57, 60-63
Bob's Pantry (Glendale, CA), 60-61
Boos, Henry, 44
Bowman, Jack, 59
Buddie's Food 'n Fun (Brooklyn, NY), 130
Bullet Drive-In (Camarillo, CA), 155
Burger Chef, 176
Burger King, 176
Burke, Stanley, 89, 92-95
Cable, Martin, 114
Car radios, 138-139
Carbonated water, 124
Carhops, 89-100
Carpenter's Drive-In (Los Angeles, CA), 73-77
Carpenter, Harry, 73-77
Carrol's, 176
Chicken in the Rough (Oklahoma City, OK), 65
Chuc Wagon, 64
Claude Federal Neon, 25, 80
Claude, Georges, 80
Coca-Cola, 33, 66-70
Coffee-shops, 159, 174-176
Conference on Natural Beauty, 160
Cramer, Keith, 176
Dairy Queen, 123
Dari-ette Drive-In (St. Paul, MN), 141
Davis, Uncle "Fletch," 49
Delligatti, Jim, 60-63
Dobbs, Harold, 178
Dogs 'n Suds, 130
Dolores Drive-In (Hollywood, CA), 114-115
Dorgan, T. A., 22-23
Doumar's Drive-In (Norfolk, VA), 146-147, 154, 183
Doumar, Abe, 112
Doumar, Albert, 112, 146-147
Doumar, George, 112

Dr Pepper, 33, 168-170
Driv-O-Matic Drive-In (Hammond, IN), 128
Drive-in theaters, 156-157
Elias Brothers, 63
Feltman, Charles, 22
Flavin, Nel, 40
Fly-In Drive-In (Elwood, IN), 120
Fone-A-Chef, 130-137
Forke, Ruth, 145
Fox, Neil, 90
French fries, 106-107
French's Mustard, 22
Frontier Drive In (Missoula, MT), 87
Geissler, Heinrich, 80
Giffy, George, 20
Googie architecture, 174
Gordy, Frank, 104-105
Green, Robert, 20
Grossman, Ralph, 38-39
Hailey, Richard, 25, 26
Hailey, Royce, 25, 28
Hamburger wrapper art, 140
Hamburgers, 48-54, 56-58
Hamwi, Ernest, 112
Handwerker, Nathan, 23
Hard Rock Cafe, 25
Hardee's, 176
Hardee, William, 176
Harry Lewis Triple XXX (Waco, TX), 118
Hart's Drive-In (Sacramento, CA), 174
Heinz ketchup, 165
Herbert's Drive-In (Los Angeles, CA), 86
Hick's Drive-In (KY), 142-143
Hines, Duncan, 118
Hoedemaker, Sydney, 86
Horlick's Malted Milk, 17
Hot dogs, 22-23
Hot rods, 144
Hughes, Ernie, 38-39
Ice cream cones, 112
Igloo Drive-In (Seattle, WA), 38-39
Ingram, Edgar Waldo "Billy," 48, 54, 59
Jackson, Reuben W., 24-25
Jacob's Pharmacy, 66
Jimbell, Jim, 166
Johnson, Ladybird, 160
Jukeboxes, 167
Katson's Drive-In (Albuquerque, NM), 2-3
Kentucky Fried Chicken, 122
Ketchup, 165
Kim's Drive-In (Waco, TX), 166
King, Andrew James, 59, 110
King, Wayne, 59
Kings-X Drive-In (Wichita, KS), 45, 59, 110-111
Kirby, Jessie G., 24-30, 33
Kobzeff, Mildred "Skeeter," 34, 37
Kroc, Ray, 120-123, 176

Lassen, Frank, 49
Lassen, Louis, 49-50
Lazenby, R. S., 168
Lewis, Harry, 118
Longpré, Ramona, 186
Louis' Lunch (New Haven, CT), 49-50
Lowndes, George S., 66
Lucas, George, 178
Lynn, C. Stephen, 135, 183
Magowan, Lorraine, 71
Malted milks, 17
Marchiony, Italo, 112
Mark's In & Out (Livingston, MT), 89
Marquee Drive-In (Mesa, AZ), 126
Marriott, J. Willard, 32, 64-73
Matchbook art, 36
McAllister, Wayne, 77-78, 83
McDonald's, 34-35, 60, 90-91, 106, 110-123, 160, 176
McDonald, "Mac" Maurice, 34-35, 37, 90, 110-123
McDonald, Richard, 34-35, 37, 90, 110-123
McDonnell's Drive-In (Los Angeles, CA), 98-99
McDonnell, Rusty, 75, 99
McNeely, Johnny, 96
Melody Lanes Drive-In (Los Angeles, CA), 86
Mels Drive-In, 176-177, 178-182, 187
Menches, Frank, 49-50, 56
Menu art, 84-85
Meston, Stanley, 90
Milkshakes, 17
Moore, D. McFarland, 80
Morris, Wanda, 147
Morrison, Wade, 168
Motormat, 121, 125
Moxie, 33
Nagreen, Charlie, 49, 56
Naylor, Tiny, 119
Neal, Margie, 96
Neon lighting, 80-83
Nora's (Minneapolis, MN), 155
Osborne, Mr. and Mrs. Beverly, 65
Ott's Drive-In (San Francisco, CA), 152-153
Paul's Drive-In (Bakersfield, CA), 72
Pemberton, Dr. John Styth, 66
Pig sandwich, 25, 28-29
Pig Stands, 12-14, 24-30, 76-77, 187
Porky's Drive-In (St. Paul, MN), 83, 108-110, 155, 175
Powell, Josephine, 89
Prohibition, 19, 31
Purdy, Kenneth C., 125
Richard's Drive-In (Cambridge, MA), 123
Roberts Brothers Drive-In (Burbank, CA), 44, 78-79
Robinson, Frank, 66

Robison, Violney, 155-158
Roen, Ted, 172-173, 187
Roller skates, 184-185
Sanders Court and Cafe (Corbin, KY), 122
Sanders, Col. Harlan, 122
Sandy's, 176
Schilling's Drive-In (KY), 136
Sill's Drive-In (Las Vegas, NV), 81, 88
Simon's Drive-In (Los Angeles, CA), 71
Simon, Bill, 75-77
Sivil's Drive-In(n) (Houston, TX), 89, 96-100, 101-103
Sivils, J. D. and Louise, 96-100, 101-103, 127
Smith, Troy N., 122, 131-136, 183
Soda fountains, 16-17, 20-21, 124
Soda jerks, 21
Sodas, 20-21
Sonic Drive-In, 131-136, 148-150, 183
Stan's Drive-In (Fresno, CA), 87, 92-95
Steak 'n Shake, 150-151, 161-164
Stephens, Ralph and Amanda, 114
Straub, O. E. "Ott," 152
Stuart's Drive-In (Houston, TX), 126-127
Stuart, R. E. "Sonny," 126-127
Sullivan, Ruth and Charles, 120
Sundaes, 20-21
Texas toast, 26
The Hot Shoppe, 72-73
The Old Corner Drugstore, 168-170
The Track Drive-In (Los Angeles, CA), 121, 125
Thomas, Frank, 176
Tik-Tok Restaurant (Portland, OR), 117
Tiny Naylors Drive-In (Hollywood, CA), 119
Top Hat Drive-In (Shawnee, OK), 122, 131-136
Truelson, Ray, 110, 175
Van de Kamp's Drive-In (Glendale, CA), 82-83
Van Hekken, Buna "Johnnie," 96-97
Varsity Drive-In (Atlanta, GA), 104-105, 183
Venable, Willis, 66
Wagner's Drive-In (St. Louis Park, MN), 44
Wagstaff, Donald, 178
Walgreen Drugs, 16, 21
Walt's Drive-In (Essex County, NJ), 4-5
Weiss, Mel, 176, 178
Weiss, Steven, 178, 187
White Castle, 48-55, 59
Wian, Robert C., Jr., 57-58, 60-63
Window serving trays, 42-45
Wolfman Jack, 139
Woodruff, Richard, 60
Wright, Frank Lloyd, 75
Wright, Frank, 32-33
Yaw's Drive-In (Portland, OR), 117
Yellow Jacket (Atlanta, GA), 104